POWER
ENCOUNTERS

OTHER BOOKS BY DR. FRANCIS J. SIZER

Into His Presence: How to Find the Ultimate Treasure

POWER

ENCOUNTERS

UNLOCKING
the Supernatural through
EXPERIENCES WITH THE HOLY SPIRIT

DR. FRANCIS J. SIZER

DESTINY IMAGE® PUBLISHERS, INC.
P.O. Box 310, Shippensburg, PA 17257-0310
"Promoting Inspired Lives"

This book and all other Destiny Image and Destiny Image Fiction books are available at Christian bookstores and distributors worldwide.

Cover design by Eileen Rockwell
Interior design by Terry Clifton

For more information on foreign distributors, call 717-532-3040.
Or reach us on the Internet: www.destinyimage.com

ISBN 13 TP: 978-0-7684-1935-1
ISBN 13 EBook:978-0-7684-4526-8
ISBN LP: 978-0-7684-4527-5
ISBN HC: 978-0-7684-4528-2

For Worldwide Distribution, Printed in the U.S.A.
3 4 5 6 / 21 20 19

Dedication

I'd like to dedicate this work to the Holy Spirit Who is my faithful Friend, my Counselor and Advocate, the One I depend upon for Guidance and Direction. He teaches me the Truth and helps me to walk in it. He gives freely of His gifts, and blesses me with Supernatural Encounters.

Acknowledgments

I'd like to acknowledge my lifetime companion and best friend, Eileen, for her constant love, support and abiding encouragement. She is brilliant and beautiful. And even more importantly, she hears the Holy Spirit like no other person I know. God truly gave me a a partner who far exceeded my expectations.

CONTENTS

Chapter 1

THE CALL

The wiry, old Irish woman lined up all eight of us children on the first day of her new job as our home cleaning lady. She wanted to meet us; and so like toy soldiers, we all stood at attention awaiting her military inspection. Without hesitation, Mary, the housemaid, pointed her long, thin finger at me as if she knew something none of us knew.

She was hired by my mother, who was pregnant at the time, to clean our large, six-bedroom house. I think we stood at attention since we were afraid of the old woman. I know I was afraid of her. I recall one time sliding down the bannister railing to avoid stepping on her newly polished steps. She was from the old school of thought, if you will. She valued authority and order and discipline at the expense of others' feelings and sensitivities. Her word was law.

As she pointed me out among my seven siblings that very first day, she stated to my mother, "This one is to be the priest."

I later recalled the prophet Samuel going to the house of Jesse because the Lord had chosen one of his sons to be successor to Saul as king of Israel. The Lord made it clear to Samuel not to look at a man's appearance, but rather to look into a man's heart. It is God's way to look at our heart. A clean and upright heart is our God's desire. Samuel looked at the seven sons of Jesse before him and his spirit was not moved to choose any.

He said to Jesse "Are these all the sons you have?" Jesse answered, "There is still the youngest tending the sheep." Samuel said, "Send for him." So he sent for him and brought him before Samuel.

> Then the Lord said, "Rise and anoint him;
> this is the one." So Samuel took the horn of
> oil and anointed him in the presence of his
> brothers, and from that day on the Spirit
> of the Lord came powerfully upon David"
> (1 Samuel 16:11-13).

Years later, this word through the old Irish Christian proved to be prophetic. I did go on and become a Roman Catholic priest. In my senior year of high school, I fought off impulses to enter the seminary, but in the end I submitted to that greater voice within pulling me in a direction I did not want to go. I took the archdiocesan entrance examination with hundreds of other candidates in 1966. Secretly, I was hoping that I would be rejected. News came that they wanted me; and because I ranked first in the entrance exam, I would be sent immediately to the Vatican in Rome for ten years of study. The thought overwhelmed me.

As the summer wore on into August, I submitted again to an inner voice that pounded in my heart. The voice was calling me to be a priest. I realized no rest would come to me until I answered this unique invitation from God. No rest would come back to my soul until I turned over my will to Him. His invitation bellowed within me the sound, "Come closer." The words of poet Francis Thompson spring to mind in his brilliant, poetic work *The Hound of Heaven:*

> *I fled Him down the nights*
> *and down the days;*
> *I fled Him down the arches of the years;*
> *I fled Him down the labyrinth*
> *ways of my own mind;*

And in the midst of tears I hid from Him...

Francis Thompson was a tortured soul, yet in spite of his madness and alcoholism this genius puts his very finger of the essence of God's desire to pierce our souls more deeply. True happiness is an illusion except in following hard after God and His path for us in life. Misery comes in following false illusions. Thompson's genius likewise awakens us to how much God is hunting for our very souls. The reason for the hunt is clear. God simply wants to be with us more than anything else. This truth is something I was to learn over the following years.

I attended the seminary thinking I would serve God and His people. I thought I could do something for God. I was wrong. He wanted to do something for me.

And so, in 1966, I entered the Catholic Seminary of the Archdiocese of Philadelphia. The model of formation at the place was more monastic and contemplative, although there was some time for sports, television entertainment, and leisure. I immediately had to address the scholarship to study in Rome. I told the deans I had to decline the honor, which would have taken me on a different path, that of administrative leadership within the church's hierarchy through the Vatican. I opted for a humbler path as a parish, church pastor by remaining at the local seminary. My interests were more along the lines of working with people in an appointed church in the archdiocese. I wanted to be with them at important moments in time like birth, illness, marriage, crisis, and death. Becoming a pastor seemed more becoming to me.

Those long years in the seminary taught me much about philosophy, theology, and the Scriptures. In 1974, I was ordained with the sacrament of Holy Orders with thirty-two other young men in the basilica of the Archdiocese of Philadelphia. My life as a priest was about to begin. The work at my first parish was good. The church where I was appointed had 2,300 families on the records. There was too much to do and too little time to do it. Preaching on Sundays was intimidating to me. Preparing an interesting sermon each week was demanding. I found I could talk about Jesus Christ and the Gospel, but something was lacking in my repertoire. The work I did in my ministry was somewhat fruitful. I worked with our school, which had more than 1,000 children enrolled.

I worked with the young, the elderly, nursing homes, hospital visitations, shut-ins, our sports programs, catechism program, and newcomers. I said Mass every day as well as officiated over baptisms, marriages, and funerals weekly. The people seemed to love me. Popularity was not a problem. Everyone loves a young, energetic priest. I should have been satisfied, but I wasn't. Things were not happening around me like in the Book of the Acts of the Apostles.

There were no miracles, signs and wonders occurring! And I realized I had a problem with leading people in prayer when I didn't seem to know God in an intimate manner.

REAL, INTIMATE LOVE

I only knew *about* Jesus—I didn't know Him personally. What I mean by this statement is that I knew I loved God and believed in a God who loved me, but I never experienced His love in the same way a person loves another. How could I know of His love for me except indirectly: through the loving parents I believed He provided; through my wonderful brothers and sisters and friends; and through all the material provisions I believed He gave me. This is how I knew He loved me indirectly.

But when someone encounters a person directly, they realize the truth about love in a different way. It becomes a whole different kind of reality. To fall in love with a person is a reaction to an emotional experience, not a case of intellectual idealism. It is no longer a matter that originates in the head or intellect. Our rationale and reason become subordinated to a chemistry dominated by feeling and irrational exuberance.

To know unconditional, consuming love is something that burns in a person's heart and is engraved upon the person's soul. It is an undeniable experience and an unforgettable memory indelibly marked in one's consciousness. This is what it means to be in love.

The moment of personal encounter is what a relationship with Jesus is all about. To really know Jesus is not to fall in love with the ideal about Him, but to actually fall in love with Him as a real person I have met. To fall in love with Jesus is not to fall in love with His teachings and then to follow them as a blueprint. It is to fall in love with Him personally, and then out of that love to follow His teachings.

This is a huge distinction that many fail to make. For example, there are those who go to church religiously on a Sunday morning because it is their routine, or it is expected of them, or it makes them feel good in serving God. Some feel by going to church they are appeasing a requirement of the commandments, which they are, but this is their sole motivation for going out of fear of not going.

The more quintessential question they need to be asking themselves should result in the fact that they want to be with the person they love most in life—namely, the Lord. Out of the relationship then comes the practice of prayer, church, and good works—the result of the love affair with the God they have personally encountered. This encounter cannot be replaced or substituted by any other person or thing this life has to offer. Jesus becomes the highest high. He is the only passion. False illusions like drugs and drink and any other kind of rush pale to the high God can provide. With David we can say:

> *Better is one day in your courts than a thousand elsewhere; I would rather be a doorkeeper in the house of my God than dwell in the tents of the wicked* (Psalm 84:10).

In the Song of Songs, the Shulammite woman is longing for her lover. She has a passionate love for the lover of her soul. Her focus is solely upon Him. Her sensitivities are totally awakened to Him. With this reality in her life now clearly defined, all else in life is vain pursuit and vanity of vanities. Once He has captured her heart, there is no turning back for her. Her only true passion is for Him. Her pursuit after Him is set in motion by His touch and presence with her. It is not set off by anything she read about Him. It is not set off by anything anyone else has told her about Him.

It all occurs when they come face to face with each other. Boundless, endless love come crashing in through the mere presence of their chemistry together. She goes on to say to Him:

> *...Your love is more delightful than wine. Pleasing is the fragrance of your perfumes; your name is like perfume poured out. No wonder the young women love you! Take me away with you—let us hurry! Let the king bring me into his chambers* (Song of Songs 1:2-4).

God desires an intimacy with Him irrespective of our gender. Passionate love for Him is therefore born out of a deep personal encounter. It is the encounter that makes it all real.

THE NEED AND HUNGER FOR MORE

The discrepancy between the reality and the ideal created a nagging tension within me. There had to be more to knowing God. There had to be more to ministry. As much as I tried to fit in with the normal duties of the priesthood like other clergy did, the more awkward and out of place I felt. I could not make this desire for more go away. Once again, that nagging feeling for more tugged at my soul. I had to have the real thing like in the days of the apostles. I had to see miracles in my life. Nothing else would bring contentment. My dissatisfaction could only be filled with more of Jesus.

When we come to a place of great need and hunger for more, this is where God comes through. One night while in prayer in my room, I wept and wept for more of God. I think I just didn't know how to get there. I didn't know how I could see miracles in my ministry. I was tired and worn out from performance. My personal performance was a type of perfectionism, especially in academics. It is not easy to be first in your class all through school. It is not easy to be valedictorian of a college and then valedictorian of a major university. But this is what I did. It won me accolades and honors in the short run, but created a problem of striving, achievement, and a false sense of self-worth.

Somehow, this plague leads ultimately to burn-out. Anyone beset like this has high expectations of self. The pressure is unbearable. In my case, each Sunday I had to top my sermon with a better and more, clever sermon every week. Thank God deliverance from this curse was not far away. God loved me not because I was so smart and clever but simply because I was His son. I knew this with my head. I was about to know it in my heart.

As the dissatisfaction with my life grew more intense, I found myself in my prayers of desperation with God. "You have to do something" I would pray over and over again. At the point of desperation and great need, we can no longer continue with the status quo. The pain of remaining the same becomes so much greater than the pain of change—even if we don't know what to expect in the change. When we have exhausted every avenue to find a better way, turned over every rock and stone, run out of options, choices, and paths to follow and pursue—it is a most uncomfortable place to be.

Our flesh, our works, and our talent that we are used to relying upon cannot create the "something new." It is beyond our grasp and beyond our resources. We want it and we want to get there, but we don't know how to do it. I wanted to see God perform miracles like in the Book of the Acts of the Apostles to help people in their lives and to show people how much God loves them. Yet I didn't know how this was possible.

I was taught in seminary that the supernatural events of signs and wonders in the Book of Acts was for that period and time alone. It was not for today. The apostles were empowered by the Holy Spirit with supernatural gifts to help the early church develop and grow. With the death of the last apostle, they taught us that all signs and wonders ceased to exist. This is the common and time-honored teaching in the Roman Catholic church except for occasional miracles here and there.

In many Evangelical churches, the teaching is even more restrictive and absolute. Signs and wonders ceased with the death of the last apostle, they say. The gifts of the Holy Spirit are no longer manifested in the church of Jesus Christ today, they teach. We don't need healing, they teach, since all emphasis is placed on the forgiveness of our sin Christ bought for us by His precious death.

With an inquisitive mind, I could not accept such rationale. Just because the twelve apostles died as men did not mean that the Holy Spirit died and left the church. Historical research is clear that miracles continued well into the third century C.E. and Christian communities thrived by faith in the Holy Spirit. The Holy Spirit promised to be with believers as a Comforter, Counselor, Teacher, and Guide. The same Holy Spirit who descended upon the 120 gathered in the upper room in fear and trembling caused them all to be brave witnesses of the Gospel on Pentecost Sunday.

All of them were filled with the Holy Spirit
and began to speak in other tongues as the
Spirit enabled them (Acts 2:4).

So it was not just the twelve filled, but all 120 gathered were filled with the power of the same Holy Spirit to preach, teach, heal, and deliver in Jesus' precious name.

What this teaches us is that we must rely upon God's Word as our standard of truth. We must pattern our Christian walk around the Word of God. Many believers healed in the New Testament beyond the apostles, like Ananias healing Saul's blindness—Saul who became the apostle Paul and shared the Good News of the Gospel with the Gentiles (Acts 9:17). What all of these believers had in common was being filled with the Holy Spirit.

More than Hope and Encouragement

Up until now when I visited people in the hospital, all I could offer was hope and encouragement for them to get better. There is nothing wrong with hope and encouragement. The way I saw it, Jesus would walk into those rooms in the hospital and heal the sick. They would recover. My blessing and smile seemed inept and insufficient. There had to be a way to get Jesus into the hospital room for a complete recovery. Everything I read about Him in the Gospel pointed to a will to heal.

> *Jesus went throughout Galilee, teaching in their synagogues, proclaiming the good news of the kingdom, and healing every disease and sickness among the people. News about him spread all over Syria, and people brought to him all who were ill with various diseases, those suffering severe pain,*

the demon-possessed, those having seizures,
and the paralyzed; and he healed them
(Matthew 4:23-24).

The night I was in prayer weeping for God to help me was not in vain. That night a peace and blessed assurance came over me like I had never known before. It was as if God was comforting me in my own room, personally telling me things were about to change. I could hear the words repeat inside me, "Do not let your heart be troubled. Have faith in God and have faith in me." My faith was about to change. It would be a faith in which I knew He lived in me and He gave me great confidence.

I prayed to God to make Himself real to me. I surrendered my life to Him that night. I ran out of gas, as I like to put it, and knew I could not go on if things didn't change. My way of living didn't work anymore. Something new had to be born inside me. My works, my strivings, my sinful habits had to be washed away. God was permitted to make me a new, clean vessel and to start over again with me. That night I was born again! I later reflected on what Jesus said in John 3:3: *"Very truly I tell you, no one can see the kingdom of God unless they are born again."*

Chapter 2

THE BAPTISM IN THE HOLY SPIRIT

About two weeks later, a group of fifteen people began to meet in the rectory basement for prayer. I was told they called themselves "charismatics." I had first heard the term back in 1968 in my college days from a seminarian from my home parish. He told me about meetings he attended that took place at Duquesne University in Pennsylvania. He said, "God really came to these meetings and spoke at them through ordinary people." I was skeptical at the time. He invited me to go with him to the prayer meetings, but I declined. Now several years later, the same type of charismatic group was meeting in my own home. In hindsight, I didn't go to God, so He came to me.

My first impression was to attend the meeting out of curiosity. I rationalized that I even had an obligation to my church to make sure these people did not present a heresy, for the greater good of my parish. So I went one night.

They all sat around in a circle of chairs. There were no prayer books on the chairs, but people spontaneously spoke out as if they were talking to God. They sang simple songs, read Scriptures from the Bible, and actually prayed effortlessly to Someone they couldn't see but believed was listening to them. There was no specific leader of the group. No one wore a Roman collar except me, yet these people genuinely seemed to be in touch with a divine presence near to them.

When the meeting was over, a few of them asked me to come again next week and share a Bible teaching for ten minutes. I asked them what would they like me to talk about and they were all in unison quick to reply, "Let the Holy Spirit lead you, Father." So with that I went about preparing a sermon for this occasion.

I believed God's lead and guidance wanted me to talk about His presence in creation. I loved science, and physics in particular. I even had developed a beautiful theory of cosmology whereby God's presence permeated all of the universe at a subatomic level. Saint Paul had beautifully expressed God's majestic presence in the first Chapter of the Book of Colossians. And so my short teaching began to develop. I would begin with a reading from the Book of Genesis and quickly move into Psalm 104, the creation psalm, and then on to my climax with Colossians 1. It was perfect.

So I went to the meeting armed with my own Bible and concordance and notes galore. One person in the group said, "Let's pray and invite the Holy Spirit to come before Father Sizer teaches us." And so we prayed. Someone else said, "I feel good tonight; let's sing about the birds of the sky and the fishes of the sea; let's sing about creation." Then another read from the Book of Genesis on creation. Then someone read Psalm 104, the creation psalm. And to top it all off, another person read from the Book of Colossians chapter 1. I jumped up out of my seat and yelled, "He's here!"

Everyone looked at me as if I had two heads. Yes, the Holy Spirit was there that night, and He went to all that trouble to show me that He is here and that He is real. You see, none of the people had any idea what I was going to talk about.

Have you ever felt like you were setup? Well, in this circumstance I felt setup by God Himself. The entire event was planned by God to show me that He is real, that these people knew Him in a personal way and could communicate with Him in a way that I only hoped to be able to do. In addition to these truths, I saw how the God of the universe, who is transcendent and awesome, could also be so close and intimate as to want to take hold of my life. Imagine that. That night in October 1975 convinced me to pursue this path until I had what they had.

HOLY SPIRIT GIFTS

I decided to participate in a Life in the Holy Spirit seminar hosted by the prayer group for anyone who wanted to attend. It was an eight-week seminar held at my church in which topics like 1) the need for forgiveness of sin; 2) Jesus as Savior; 3) the Holy Spirit; and 4) Transformation of Life were all covered in detail. Scripture references were included for every week. Then on the seventh week, group leaders were to lay hands and pray for the baptism. The first baptism was unto repentance of sin; while the second baptism was a baptism of fire to empower a born-again believer in the gifts of the Holy Spirit.

The Book of Acts is clear on the distinction between water baptism and the baptism in the Holy Spirit. Luke records people already water baptized in the name of Jesus were then prayed over by Peter and John for the baptism of the Holy Spirit (Acts 8:9-19). It is the baptism of water that provides a model for Christian initiation. Jesus believed in the baptism of water for repentance. He believed in the baptism of the Holy Spirit as a baptism of empowerment. John the Baptist even realized this distinction. He writes:

> *I baptize you with water. But one who is more powerful than I will come, the straps of whose sandals I am not worthy to untie. He will baptize you with the Holy Spirit and fire* (Luke 3:16).

It is both the forgiveness and power of the Holy Spirit that are the vital factors in Christian initiation. As a Roman Catholic member, I received infant baptism; and when twelve years old, received the ritual of the sacrament of Confirmation from a bishop in a ceremony with fifty-five other classmates.

Both events strengthened my standing in the church and likely somewhat strengthened my belief in Christ. These actions were rituals or signs that lacked any real power therein. Dedicating an infant baby into a believing and supporting family is a good thing. But each one of us born into this world must make a decision for or against Christ. As an adult, I needed to make my own personal commitment to Jesus as my Savior. It had to become my choice.

Now at this point I needed a real strengthening in the Holy Spirit. The ritual at twelve years old did little to nothing to change me. The real fire of the Holy

Spirit, I now believed, could bring the change I was looking for. It was right around the corner.

I was beginning to realize as the leader in my parish that although I had spent years and years in the seminary, although I was finally ordained as a Roman Catholic priest, it didn't make any difference in my relationship with God. I know I loved God. What I learned is that I didn't know that He loved me. That love only comes through a personal encounter and relationship with the God who does love us. Second, I was aware without the shadow of a doubt that my ministry needed to be empowered by the Holy Spirit in order to be supernaturally effective. I wanted to do the same things that Jesus did.

After all, it is Jesus who says:

> *These signs will accompany those who believe: In my name they will drive out demons; they will speak in new tongues; they will pick up snakes with their hands; and when they drink deadly poison, it will not hurt them at all; they will place their hands on sick people, and they will get well* (Mark 16:17-18).

I wasn't planning to pick up snakes or drink poison to test God in His word, but I did expect to see people healed when I prayed with them. When I went to visit the sick in the hospital, I would bless them in a prayer, and nothing evident happened in terms of their physical condition ever. It was a frustrating and awkward situation time after time. Why didn't my prayers work? Why didn't the people recover and the sick get well? Was something lacking in my prayer or my belief or the patient's belief? I knew something was not right, and I was very determined to find an answer.

THE GREATEST NIGHT OF MY LIFE

I found the Life in the Spirit seminar refreshing and simple in its teaching. All of it built up to the night hands were laid for the Holy Spirit to come. Let me tell you about that night—November 5, 1975. It was to be the greatest night of my entire life! Three people prayed with me. Their prayer asked Jesus to send the Holy Spirit upon me. Then they prayed in tongues, their own prayer language, asking Him to baptize me in the Holy Spirit. My body began to shake. I shook and shook more as convulsions of power overcame my body. I shook off the seat of the front pew of the church. I could see the fear in the eyes of the people praying for me. I then screamed out, "Stop it, stop it!" But it didn't stop. Instead, the waves of convulsions got stronger and stronger.

Power went through me in waves of electricity. The electricity coursed through me as I bounced off the floor time and time again. This went on for thirty minutes to an hour, I don't know exactly the time. As I got more used to the electrical impulses, I noticed they were accompanied by feelings of love. It was like liquid love pulsating through my entire being, penetrating even to my heart and my deepest recesses. The love was nothing I had ever felt before—so very intense. The love could only be spelled "LOVE."

It was God's love pouring through my soul. I then was able to hear the words in my head resound, "You were here all this time and I never knew You. You loved me from the beginning like this and I never knew." What an incredible revelation. What an unbelievable experience. As the shaking finally began to subside, tears welled up from the deepest part of my soul. I cried out loud with tears bellowing from my heart. I felt God's love consume me in fire.

I thought how great He is to even care about me. I knew this instantly. I knew He loved me. I knew He forgave me. I knew He was washing me clean from all my sin and strivings for perfection. I knew I was accepted by Him as I was, not as I ought to be. I knew I was free from the past and free from myself. He erased in a moment's time with His passionate love all my former hurts and pain. It was miraculous. I wailed out loud, filling the entire church with my cries. I didn't care what the other people thought. My focus was on the Holy Spirit who changed me. Many might perceive this as an embarrassing moment and perhaps it was. But I physically felt God rearranging my gut, and out of my belly flowed rivers of living water. It all became true. His word became true. I was a new creation.

The third phase of this experience now began. The tears subsided after another thirty minutes to an hour. I felt physically numb. It was like that feeling of pins and needles throughout my body. I lack for words to describe it. An anointing of God's presence was left on me. It was a tangible aura emanating off my being, yet through my being too. Both my hands were now extremely hot to the touch. My face must have looked angelic because I felt a light released from my eyes. I was then drawn up into another dimension. I was no longer conscious of my earthly surroundings. I began to hear the most beautiful music draw me toward it and away from earthly limitations.

The music was choirs of angels singing in unison as my gaze went toward a golden, yellowish, white light. I knew it was the cloud of God's glory. I knew I was in the presence of Greatness. It was the closest thing I could imagine to Heaven. This rapture lasted another thirty minutes to an hour on earth. It only seemed like a brief second of time in heaven. All time is suspended there. There is only the conception of the present. Even following my return to my body in the church I had perfect peace.

What happened to me that night was not expected by me. I could never have dreamed it or anticipated it. I never thought any of that were possible. Yet it happened. All the others received prayer and most began to pray in tongues. No one shook. My prayer language came to me a few days before they laid hands on me. I prayed well into the night in my new prayer language and maintained a closeness to God I wanted forever.

THE FIRE OF GOD

There were 120 people baptized in the Spirit that night in my church. This is precisely the same number of people gathered in the upper room for the day of Pentecost. The number has great significance. In Genesis, Noah finished construction on of the ark after 120 years. This marked the end of the age of man and the works of his flesh, and the beginning of the age of the Spirit of God. God says in Genesis:

> *My Spirit will not contend with humans forever, for they are mortal; their days will be a hundred and twenty years* (Genesis 6:3).

What God is telling us is that the labors of our flesh are in vain, while with His help in the Holy Spirit our work will be fruitful and lasting.

The next day I tried to make sense of what happened the night before. None of the charismatic leadership could help me. No one had an explanation for what happened to me. So I researched historically the baptism of the Holy Spirit in early American revivals. I came across the story of Charles G. Finney from the nineteenth century.

Finney faced the question of leaving ministry, like I did, because he didn't see the power of the Gospel. If he couldn't have the Jesus of the Gospel, he would leave pastoring and pursue a worldly course of life. He decided, like me, to cry out to God for more. Finney writes in his autobiography:

> As I turned and was about to take a seat by the fire, I received a mighty baptism of the Holy Spirit. Without any expectation of it, without ever having the thought in my mind that there was such a thing for me, without any memory of ever hearing the thing mentioned by any person in the world, the Holy Spirit descended upon me in a manner that seemed to go through body, soul and me.

I could feel the impression, like a wave of electricity, going through me and through me. Indeed, it seemed to come in waves of liquid love, for I could not express it in any other way. It seemed like the very breath of God. I can distinctly remember that it seemed to fan me like immense wings. No words can express the wonderful love that was spread abroad in my heart. I wept aloud with joy and love. I literally bellowed out the unspeakable overflow of my heart. The waves came over me one after another until I remember crying out, "I shall die if these waves continue; I cannot bear anymore."[1]

Finney's words brought me so much peace and satisfaction. I had an experience with the Holy Spirit identical to his experience with God. We both found ourselves immersed in the baptism of fire. Even our recounting of the experience is identical. I was not crazy. I was not mentally ill. I was perfectly sane with a supernatural experience few have ever experienced. What a privilege.

The morning after the experience, the fire of God was still upon me. I was filled up from the soles of my feet to the crown of my head with a liquid love and fire. My hands were on fire and my body was burning. Let me be clear that it was anything but uncomfortable.

It was heavenly. I knew I was different now; a better change I could never have dreamed of. I was like a burning bush that wouldn't be consumed. My hands in particular were burning from within.

The Holy Spirit now surged through me. I walked in an anointing that could see through people. By this I mean that I knew things about people that I shouldn't have known. But I had a "knowing" without a sense of judging anyone in a bad light. I knew people's sins; I knew people's intent. I knew just what to do and what not to do. The confessional lines grew longer every week as people came to hear the priest tell them their sins before they could ever confess them to him. It was not unusual for me to hear confessions and give advice for five to six hours every Saturday.

When I walked down the mall, for example, as I passed people, I knew about their health conditions, their ages, and even problems they were dealing with privately. What was going on with me? What was to be the purpose of this knowledge?

A SHAKING

God has done a shaking in me. I thought of the word in the Book of Hebrews

At that time his voice shook the earth,
but now he has promised, "Once more I

will shake not only the earth but also the heavens." The words "once more" indicate the removing of what can be shaken—that is, created things—so that what cannot be shaken may remain (Hebrews 12:26-27).

"The words 'once more' indicate the removing of what can be shaken—that is, created things—so that what cannot be shaken may remain"—namely God. Let me also say this shaking is not to be confused with shaking that sometimes occurs during deliverance prayer. This experience was purely an overwhelming emergence into the power of God.

I remember a humorous story about our school kids coming to the church building for confession. There were 1,250 children in our elementary and middle school. That is a lot of kids for individual confession. The confessional room was modernized with two chairs facing each other. The old confession screen separating the priest and the penitent was done away with for the children. The priest was to extend his hand over the penitent and pray for absolution of sin.

Remember, my hands were now red hot. The first child came in and told her sins. I extended my hand over her and immediately she fell under the power of God in the chair. I didn't know what to do. I had heard about being "slain in the Spirit" or "resting in the Spirit," and now it happened in my confessional! So I picked up the child and put her in the corner of the room to rest, then opened the door and brought in the next child. The same thing happened to her as with four more kids until I ran out of space to put the unconscious children. Sister Superior was wondering where her children were. Ha! God certainly has a sense of humor. The power of God causes all flesh to bow unto Him. No flesh may stand in His awesome presence.

ENDNOTE

1.   Helen Wessel, ed., *The Autobiography of Charles G. Finney* (Bloomington, MN: Bethany House Publishers, 2006).

Chapter 3

THE POWER TO HEAL

I couldn't wait to start praying for the sick at our area hospital where I regularly visited parishioners who were sick. I joke now that patients at Fitzgerald Mercy Hospital used to see me coming with the "Last Rites," and they would run the other way because they knew my showing up meant they were about to die. But that reputation was about to change.

One day I visited a 65-year-old woman named Anne who was dying with stage four cancer. During that time people, in general, with a terminal condition stayed in the hospital to die. Insurance companies didn't chase them out. Anne was put on morphine to kill the pain of the cancer. The family and staff of the hospital knew she was about to die. The smell of death filled the air in the private room. I stepped over to her, knowing the Holy Spirit was with me. I prayed over the woman by casting out the spirit of death and the spirit of cancer in Jesus' name.

Her eyes grew enormously wide as the miraculous power of God went through my right hand into her body. I commanded her to get up out of bed and walk with me down the corridor. As we walked, she got visibly stronger and stronger. The nursing staff came running toward us and shouted to the woman, "What are you doing out of bed? Get back in bed now." I smiled at the woman and it put her at ease as we returned to the room. The nurse wanted to know what had happened. I told her I prayed for a miracle. She said that she would have to get the doctor.

As the story unfolded, the woman's health was so drastically different that the doctors retested her and could find no cancer in her body. She was discharged a day or two later with a clean bill of health and a love for God that was stronger than ever. She was instrumental in witnessing to her miracle at my first healing service a few months later.

Word of the miracle spread throughout the hospital and throughout my parish. There was a buzz in the air. Whenever I went back to the hospital to visit the sick after the news of the miracle, pairs and groups of hospital staff would follow me to catch a glimpse at what God's miracle power would do next.

I now found myself doing what Jesus did in His public ministry. No longer did I have to resort to feeble, empty prayers or words that lacked the power of God within. Now, I could witness with my own eyes the healing works of God.

Another woman desperately sought prayer for her sister. She said her sister, Dee, had just been diagnosed with a large tumor set behind her optic nerve that caused her to lose her eyesight. Dee was given three months to live without any hope for survival. The tumor was growing at a fast rate—it was deemed inoperable. Dee had three children and a husband she was not prepared to leave behind. I agreed to pray with her. When she arrived at the rectory, her sister guided Dee into my office. The office staff was situated across from my office so all four of them saw the blind woman guided into my office. I shut the door to talk to Dee. I asked her if she believed in miracles. I could see she had faith to be healed. I remember the sunlight beaming brightly through the window that late morning.

I laid my hands over her head. I prayed for Jesus to crush the tumor and cause it to be no more. The power had gone through my hot hands and into her head. The tumor was gone. I couldn't see it but I knew from God it was gone. I then had Dee open her eyes to see out the window into the bright sunshine morning. She did. She saw. It was another miracle, this time in the rectory office. Dee, a middle-age Italian woman, would not stop covering me with kisses and hugs. She exuberantly said, "Wait until I tell my children!" She was healed. A death sentence turned into a new lease on life. As I opened the door, the two sisters hugged and cried together. My office staff stared with dropped jaws at what had happened.

Two miracles occurred that day. One miracle was that the tumor was completely gone in seconds and the woman's eyesight was restored. But there was another miracle that some of my staff had to wrestle with because of what happened. The second miracle was the challenge presented to my staff. We all saw the woman come into the rectory blind; but she left the rectory thirty minutes later being able to see. What do they do with what they witnessed? Three believed, changed, and joined the prayer group; one remained the same and would not talk about it again. The second miracle is giving spiritual sight to faith.

SPIRITUAL SIGHT TO FAITH

I ask you, "What do you do with this true story?" It is so out of the norm of reality, but it happened. Many people tend to reject things that don't fit into their reality. If they haven't experienced it, then it doesn't exist. These kinds of things make them very uncomfortable and unnerved. I understand this. People like routine and predictability.

But Jesus does upset the applecart. He does change our reality. He broadens the possibilities of what can be and takes us into dimensions of new realities. When Dee walked out that office door, my staff was confronted with going with the new reality or rejecting it. In Jesus' day, the same decision had to be made. The majority of the common people wanted miracles and believed. The religious leaders tried to find reasons to condemn Jesus' miracles and healings because it played into changing everything they had built up in their self-righteous belief system. They were comfortable with the status quo and established in their minds complete control over their own reality. In two thousand years' time, some thinking has not changed.

Some people embraced what I embarked on in healing, while others were set against it and used all of their power to debunk, discredit, and defame me in the future. In my naiveté, I had little insight into what lay ahead.

More than forty years have passed since this miracle occurred. I have many more to tell you about. But recently a woman came to one of my healing services who was present that day when the blind woman with the tumor was healed. At that time, Margaret was a high school student working for us by answering phone calls and office filing. She told me about the positive influence I had on her life at sixteen years of age in following Jesus. She now works in the corporate world, in IT as a chief operating officer, and is extremely successful as a business person. Yet even with that she says her greatest asset is knowing Jesus, crediting my boldness and obedience in following hard after the Lord, which ultimately led to healing Dee that day.

Margaret thanked me for my sacrifices because she knows the road has not been easy. She said the world can accept what Jesus says up to a point. To be a Christian saved from sin by grace is tolerable and even acceptable in our country. But to believe in healing, signs and wonders is just plain absurd to most.

GOD SPEAKS AND HEALS

Another change that took place inside me was how I now could hear God speaking to me very clearly in my spirit. I didn't hear an audible voice but rather I heard my own voice with a new certainty. I learned to trust my instincts and discernment, which clearly had God's success written all over it, when, I chose to follow it. And when I didn't, I clearly had my share of failure and confusion.

The Spirit of God told me it was not enough for Him to heal people here and there. He wanted me to gather people together in a healing service. The sick and those with ailments and diseases could come into one place and we could pray to the Lord to heal them. Never before in our area was anything like this seen or heard of. Personally, I had seen on television clips of Oral Roberts' healing meetings, but beyond that, I had no conception of what it would look like.

I announced at our prayer group that healing gatherings would begin the next month. It was basically a time of honoring the Lord Jesus as Healer. I emphasized to the people that I was not a healer. All honor and glory for any miracle would go to Him.

The first night of the healing service, more than 1,000 people attended. The second month, more than 2,000 people attended. The church was packed. People came two hours early for good seats. The parking lot was jammed. We were overwhelmed by the needs of people. Prayer requests came to the rectory by the hundreds. I organized my prayer team into groups of ushers, parking attendants, music ministry, prayer teams, nursing staff, etc. Buses brought people from long distances. The people showed up because they knew God would show up. The healing services became the largest Roman Catholic charismatic gathering in the entire nation from 1976 to 1982.

Following the first night's service, the Lord spoke the most wonderful words to me. It was as clear as any person speaking to me. He said, "Thank you, Frank, for giving Me an opportunity to show My people how much I love them."

In other words, He is saying to each of us that when we provide a chance for Him to love and work for others, He does. Our job is to set out and risk doing something we have never done before. It does take faith and boldness. I was stepping out over my head and standing in faith that my God would come through and bless the people. He did. He healed hundreds of people every month. Let me share with you some of the healings and miracles to build up your faith.

TRUE STORIES

One woman came down the church aisle with her German shepherd seeing-eye dog. She was totally blind from birth. Because she never had sight, it would take a creative miracle from God to give her sight. When she was about fifteen feet away from me, the dog fell down under the power of God. That's right, the German shepherd was slain in the spirit! All were watching and gasped as the woman stumbled to the ground. An assistant of mine thought this happened to protect me from the dog if it got upset at me when her master was prayed for. However, I think the more important reason the dog was slain is because God wants us to let go of everything we are dependent on so that when we come to Him we come with empty hands. The dog acted as the blind woman's eyes. She had to let go of the dog and come to Him as she was. This is an important teaching in the realm of divine healing.

I laid hands on the woman's eyes after I put my saliva on my thumbs. I believe in doing what Jesus did every step of the way. Jesus put saliva on the blind man's eyes at Bethsaida (see Mark 8:22-23). So I did too. The anointing power of the Holy Spirit went through my thumbs into her eyes and she fell to the ground slain in the Holy Spirit. When she got up, she looked at me and said she could see shadows, light, and lines. I recalled Jesus praying with the blind man who, after Jesus prayed the first time, saw people who *"look like trees walking around"* (Mark 8:24).

So I prayed a second time just as He did. This time her eyes were opened and sight was restored; she saw everything clearly. Tears rolled down the elderly woman's cheeks. She touched my face with her hands and smiled. God had done a miraculous work for her. She saw for the first time in her life!

Another remarkable miracle occurred in a ten-year-old boy born without an eardrum in his right ear, which caused deafness. The mother brought him to the healing service because she wanted prayer for the surgery to try to graft a plastic-type eardrum inside the boy's ear. The family happened to be sitting in the front row, and during the service I walked down to greet each one of them. As I touched the boy's hand, power went out from me. He immediately heard a popping sound in his right ear. The boy tugged his mother's arm and told her that he could hear and that it was loud. The mother took him to the ear surgeon who examined his ear. To his amazement, he saw a completely perfect eardrum in the right ear where there was none.

He told the boy's mother that the surgery was canceled; the boy didn't need it. Julius Neumann, MD, credited God for the miracle. In my experience, it is refreshing to find a medical person who will credit God, so I put his name here. He wrote me a letter congratulating me on my work and inquired about my technique. He happened to be a prominent physician of Jewish background, so he had no understanding of Christian healing. But who really did have any understanding of this kind of happenstance?

I prayed in front of 2,000 people for a tall man who was bent over in crippling pain. He struggled to get out of the pew as he sat on the end seat in excruciating agony. The man was a well-known television and radio personality with the ARCO Go Patrol. John flew a helicopter and reported traffic flow especially during the rush hours. Unfortunately, he was involved in a crash that he survived, but with serious consequences. He broke his neck and back in several places and was put on very strong dosages of painkillers.

I asked the six-foot-four-inch tall man to remove the head brace and back brace holding him together. I could see he had the faith to be healed. I could also see people questioning my bold action and instruction to him. I stretched out my hand, and the huge man crashed to the floor as the power of God moved over him. He was completely still on the floor of the church. I am sure some thought he would now be paralyzed from the fall. But I knew God was in control. He then rose on his own with tears in his eyes—completely restored and without any pain. He was able to return to his work flying the helicopter, which he told me he thought he would never do again. From reports I received later, he worked for another twenty years not missing a beat. God was on the move healing His people.

I have prayed with many, many people who have come out of wheelchairs because of arthritic joints and limbs, rheumatism pain, muscular weakness and degeneration, osteoporosis, enlarged hearts that have shrunk, and old age. But what I am about to tell you was something I had never seen or witnessed before.

I walked over to a woman during the healing service who was in a wheelchair in front of the 2,000 people. I believed the Holy Spirit led me to her. She was young, in her twenties. Something terrible had happened to her. I said to her, "The Lord is pleased that you came tonight." I told her that He knew of her desire to get out of the chair and move again. I then said, "You were paralyzed from being in a car accident two and half years ago." The only way I knew this is through the Holy Spirit telling me to say these things.

The Holy Spirit led me to place the middle finger of my right hand on her vertebrae exactly at the point where her spinal cord had been severed in half. She was a paraplegic. As I placed my finger on the spine, the power of electricity jolted out from my finger and instantly knit together her spinal cord! The heat was only for a second or two, but it was enormously hot. I then held her hand in mine and told her, "In the name of Jesus, rise up and walk." Her legs were very thin and atrophied, but she trusted me and trusted Jesus to give her the strength to walk.

Remember, she could not move the lower part of her body at all—not even a twinge of movement in over two years. Yet she stood up and walked with me about thirty feet across the front of the church. Thunderous applause followed the woman's efforts. Six months later I officiated at her wedding; in that same church, she walked down the aisle with her father by her side. She was married, standing and walking on her own, with no remnants of being paralyzed. This was an incredible moment.

GOD'S WILL IS TO HEAL

Some might think that it was God's will for her to be in a wheelchair for the rest of her life. But this is not my belief. I believe God's will is to heal. And that is what He was doing through me.

I have seen the Lord Jesus heal paralyzed hands and arms and lengthen legs. The most remarkable miracle of this sort occurred when the Holy Spirit showed me a visual image of a person's foot He wanted to heal. He then showed me where it was in the building and led me over to the person through hundreds and hundreds of others. He took me exactly to the woman who crashed to the floor under the power of God as I approached.

I looked down at her foot and couldn't believe what I saw. She was wearing a specially designed shoe to fit a club foot. I didn't ask her, but I knew she had been born with this deformity. I instructed the assistants to take off the boot from her foot. It exposed a stump of a foot with the toes deformed and tucked under the foot without life and movement. They were immove-able like a petrified rock. At this point, I knew the Holy Spirit brought me to her. And I realized the Holy Spirit only showed me an image of a foot, not a club foot, because I might not have the faith in God to heal her.

So I placed my two hands around her deformed foot. My hands grew red hot in time. I can never remember them being hotter. The energy and power went out of my hands into the foot. Hundreds of people stood around us, some watching, hopefully some supporting me. I literally felt bones moving in my hands and tissue softening. Bones shifted and tissue moved into their proper place. All the while, the lady was out in the Holy Spirit, not aware of what was happening. Then the unthinkable occurred. The toes came to life underneath the foot and burst forth together in one motion, then tucked underneath again. Moments later they burst forth again, and this time came into normal position, pink and supple, each toe with complete movement and freedom!

When the healing was complete, I fell to the ground exhausted and depleted. The energy the miracle took left me drained. A couple of men had to carry me back to the rectory. But praise God, this story of the club foot healing was told and retold by hundreds who witnessed it. As a matter of fact, one of my nieces was present that night. Patty was about nine years of age at the time, and she has never forgotten that amazing night, which undeniably led her to believe in miracles.

COOL WINDS FROM HEAVEN

Every healing service was different from the one before. It never became predictable or routine in any way. The Word of God says that the Spirit of God moves when and where He wills. I learned to wait on the Lord and depend on the Holy Spirit for all our needs. In one moment He is here and in the next moment He is there. *"The wind blows wherever it pleases. You hear its sound, but you cannot tell where it comes from or where it is going..."* (John 3:8). You cannot contain or capture the Holy Spirit by ritual or some automatic formula of prayer.

Our huge church was not air conditioned. We had some large fans to blow air on people, but when it got hot, the church building became stiflingly oppressive. With more than 2,000 people packed inside this hot box, well you can imagine what it was like one summer night. I was about to send everyone home and cancel the healing service. I was extremely frustrated. The leadership and even the nursing staff came to me for a decision to close the meeting. People would get sick and the already sick would get sicker because of the heat. Before I called off the meeting, I went to a part of the sacristy to be alone.

I cried out to God in frustration saying, "Why don't You do something about this heat. All the people are here for You. I'm going to send them all home." Then I heard the Spirit of God say to me, "Why don't you do something about it? Why don't you pray for a miracle? Don't you know that I have all power over nature, the winds, and the weather?"

So I told the leadership we were going on with the meeting. I stepped out to the center of the church and took the microphone. People were fanning themselves with booklets trying to cool down. I was not afraid about what I was about to do. I told them in ordinary circumstances we would have to close down the service tonight. But because we believed in miracles, we were not closing down but would now pray for God to come and air condition the entire church for the night.

I invited those who had faith to believe to join me in a short prayer. I prayed to the heavenly Father our intent and request. Then I led the people in my prayer language as the Holy Spirit gave me utterance. The people's voices and songs rose up with mine. We filled the church with prayer and praise to our great God and Father. As we did, the chandeliers and lighting fixtures on the ceiling began to blow! A mighty wind blew through the entire church. The people broke into applause for what the Lord had done. The prayer was answered. I laughed at what God had done—enjoying the cool breeze. It was totally crazy. Although still in the 90 degrees outside the building, inside it was a cool, comfortable temperature! How did He do it? I was amazed along with all the people. This was a night we would never forget.

ILLNESS AND DISEASE BE GONE

I have had the privilege to see God heal cancers hundreds of times. I have seen extreme fever and mysterious viruses on a baby in an incubator and life support instantly break by the anointing of the Holy Spirit. God has used my hands to heal diabetes, lupus erythematosus, lyme disease, burned skin tissue, chronic fatigue syndrome, meningitis, kidney disease, stomach ulcers, heart disease ailments, multiple sclerosis, leukemia, blood clots coughed up, incurable cancers, tumors literally falling off the body and other diseases healed in Jesus' Precious Name. I have seen the Spirit of God touch and heal backs and necks in seconds. People with respirators and oxygen tanks because of lung disease and emphysema have been healed immediately by God.

I prayed for children with attention deficit hyperactivity disorder (ADHD) and they were healed. There is nothing too great for God. After all, He is the One who created us. A special little girl came to a service with her mother, Margie. She simply wanted her daughter to fit in better at her special school since she was unable to keep up with the other children. The mother told me she was tested with a 65 IQ, so she was very mentally challenged. I prayed and laid hands on the child's head. I received a phone call from the mother two weeks later. She reported that the school nurse said she was doing so much better but didn't understand why the child was behaving so differently. She was joining in with other children and now even taking the lead. The mother had the school psychologist retest the girl. Her IQ rose to normal at 100. All of this by the hand of God!

Another astounding miracle occurred when a young mother brought an infant before the crowds of people for a miracle. The baby suffered from a hydrocephalic condition (water on the brain). I saw the compassion the mother had for her infant girl, so I laid hands on the child's head, which was nearly the size of the rest of the baby's body. I prayed that the Lord would take away the water from the brain. Down, down, and down the little baby's head decreased in size. That fast! It was normal size. Where the water went, I don't know. God did another supernatural sign and wonder! The healing spared the mother's infant of surgeries and probably lifetime deformity. The miracle was clear evidence of God's loving will to heal.

Although the Archdiocesan religious leaders tried in different ways to shut down the healing services many times, reports of the miracles spread far and wide across the United States. During one of several times I was summoned before the authorities, I was asked by the Cardinal Archbishop John Krol, "Father Sizer, who appointed you with this healing work? I didn't." I replied to him, "No, you didn't. God did." I appealed to a higher authority. He had no response. Better to obey God than man.

As new traveled about what God was doing, a family came from Arkansas. The parents flew their eight-year-old son to the healing service. He was literally dying from brain cancer. Their only hope was in the Lord for a cure. I took the boy aside and spoke with him. I stooped down so that I would be on the same level as the boy. I remember his eyes were lifeless, his head was bald from the chemotherapy treatments. I asked Joey if he knew Jesus and then asked him whether he believed Jesus could heal him. He said, "Yes." I laid hands over his head and the power of God poured into his body. I then told Joey to play a game every night before he went to sleep. The game would be played like this: I had him visualize the good cells in his brain eating up the cancer cells. I said, "Do this until Jesus tells you to stop." Six months later, the family returned from Arkansas. Joey had his hair and now had a twinkle in his eyes. He was free from the astroblastoma and from all cancer. Jesus had healed him.

Not all of the healing was physical in nature. God freed many from spiritual, emotional, and mental bondage and sin. I remember especially one Italian man who knelt as he watched with his own eyes these miraculous wonders of God and all he could do was weep and weep. He told God he was so sorry for his sins and promised God he would become a good father and husband. The next healing service, he brought his wife and all five sons and daughters. The entire family gave their lives to Jesus that night and promised to serve the Lord.

I recall a persistent woman literally pulling at my clothes at the end of a service to get me to pray for her need. She was not to be denied. She pressed in like the woman in the Gospel who pressed in to Jesus. Both of her hands were crippled from arthritis. I spoke a supernatural word of knowledge saying, "You harbor jealousy toward her sister," who was there with her, "and anger toward your deceased mother." I told her she had held resentment in her heart for many years.

She turned toward her sister and asked for her forgiveness for being jealous. Both had tears in their eyes. I then said, "In the name of Jesus, stretch out your hands." Immediately, her fingers and hands opened up, free from all effects from arthritis.

I could relate many other accounts of healing from depression, anxiety, and the scars of sexual abuse. I have witnessed the Lord set people free several times from the bondage of addiction to drugs and alcohol and prescription drugs. For with the Lord, nothing is impossible!

I need to tell you about one other miracle before I close this Chapter. This one had a profound effect on my personal life for reasons you will see. Eileen was an extremely talented professional ballerina and actress. She traveled overseas in the summer singing and dancing in performances. It was during one of these tours that she was sold into white slavery in Izmir, Turkey, in 1976. Because she would not comply with the wishes of the Turkish men in the nightclubs, she was virtually starved in unsanitary conditions.

With the help of the American Embassy, she managed to escape and return stateside in poor health. It was found through x-rays that Eileen suffered from eleven bleeding ulcers. Surgery was ordered to remove three-fourths of her stomach. I was called in by her mother to pray for her. As I laid hands over her stomach, the anointing power of God went out of me. It went into her stomach as she felt it tangibly touch her.

Shortly after, she was scheduled for the surgery in the hospital. Eileen insisted that the surgeon perform an endoscopic exam before he would cut. As he peered inside her stomach, he saw that all of the eleven ulcers were gone and replaced by, in his words, tissue that looked like "a newborn babe." He emerged from the operating room and shook my hand. I will never forget what this dear man said to me. He wanted to know more about my "technique." Praise God! Little did I realize at the time that God had brought Eileen into my life to be my future soul mate and loving wife.

Chapter 4

THE ENEMY AWAKENS

I have said in the past that the population's belief in the realm of the demonic is inversely proportional to the number of degrees one has hanging on their office wall. At one time I was among the unbelievers. Truth be told, I have five higher education accredited degrees and two more board certifications. So if the above premise be true, then I would likely be listed among the top disbelievers in demons. On face value it seems archaic, primitive, and completely unorthodox to propose that demons are for real. Maybe for medieval society it helped make some sense out of reality. But for those who live in the twenty-first century, it is nothing more than a primeval category of fairytale and fantasy, which has no place in today's world.

In 1973, the popular horror movie *The Exorcist* portrayed a young girl possessed by an evil entity. Two Jesuit priests were corralled to try to free the girl from the devil. Both are killed in the attempt as they prayed the Roman Rite of Exorcism. The girl is finally set free. The movie made for terrific drama and suspense. But did the movie have any credible roots in real life? According to author William Peter Blatty, the story for his book was based on a real exorcism that occurred in St. Louis, Missouri, on a young boy. One of the priests in attendance at the actual exorcism in 1949, Fr. Walter Halloran S.J., acted as an on-set advisor for the movie at Georgetown University.

I am not writing to convince anyone about the reality of demons. What I can do is to speak from my own experiences and allow readers to draw their own conclusions. I can also state that Jesus Himself believed in the reality of demons and the devil. Some might say that He accommodated to the culture, practices, and beliefs of the times 2,000 years ago.

But my understanding of Jesus is that He acquiesced to no one. He tells things like they are. If He believed in demons and cast them out of persons, then maybe our understanding of mental health practice is what is lacking, not the practice of Jesus.

Spiritual warfare is a central theme of the Gospel of Christ. When Jesus died on the cross, He descended into hell, signifying His victory over sin, death, and evil. The public ministry of Jesus was likewise tied to two key elements: 1) the proclamation of the good news that the Kingdom of God had come; and 2) the demonstration of the Kingdom's power through the casting out of demons. The sacred Scriptures back up the reality of evil.

Power over the enemy illustrates that the two kingdoms are diametrically opposed to one another. The Kingdom of God is in direct opposition to the Kingdom of darkness. The sacrifice of Jesus on the cross represents the ultimate victory of the Kingdom of God over the kingdom of evil. Every believer must take this truth and apply it to their circumstances for victory.

For believers to overcome, they must recognize this truth and apply it just as the Israelites applied the blood to the door post on the first Passover in Egypt. Why apply it if Christ already won victory for us? It is because demons are very legalistic. They know their rights, and they know when their rights are stripped from them. Casting out demons should be a common, ordinary work of a believer.

It is true this belief in demons can be taken to an extreme. There is not a demon behind every bush. But I do believe the ministry of deliverance has been abdicated by the church at large. It was provided for by Jesus so we may have freedom from bondage.

Truth needs to be restored to its proper place. The expelling of demons was an ordinary part of the ministry of Jesus. Delivering the oppressed should be a normal part of our ministry, too. To call on the blood of Jesus and to pray in the power of the blood of Jesus will revolutionize your life and calling. The precious blood of Jesus (1 Pet. 1:19) cannot be evaluated in human terms. It is priceless. Demons tremble at the utterance of the words. It is God's price for the redemption of the whole human race for all time.

THREAT TO THE ENEMY

There was a time when I didn't believe in demons. It was before I was saved and before I was baptized in the Holy Spirit. Those two events changed everything. All my existing profound theological categories and beautifully designed philosophical platforms were destroyed. The Lord brought me back to the simplicity of the Gospel. Jesus saves because Jesus just saved me. Before the power of God came upon me, I was not a threat to the enemy. When I was saved and filled with the Holy Spirit, I became a threat to the enemy.

Another way to look at this is to envision a hunter with shotgun in a high field of grassland with his dog.

Although there is no sign at all of any life in the grass-lands, when the dog is released to advance after the prey of ducks, dozens and dozens of ducks are flushed out, frantically flying away. The same holds true in the realm of spiritual warfare. There is no cause or reason for the devil to show his hand until somebody believes he is there and comes after him or comes after what he protects as his own. As soon as I used my gift of healing for the church, I became a marked man and an adversary for the devil to attack.

Several times was my life threatened. Once while returning from a healing meeting in New Jersey, in which God's glory showed forth many signs and wonders, my car's steering wheel was pulled supernaturally to the right to run my car off the Walt Whitman bridge in Philadelphia. I had no control over the steering wheel whatsoever. The car's tires ran into the guardrail on the right side, but as I called out the name of Jesus, the steering wheel was released. I sat there with my heart in my throat overlooking a 300-foot plunge into the Delaware River. Psalm 91 came to mind where it is written, *"If you make the Most High your dwelling, He will command His angels to guard you in all your ways."*

On another occasion, my car was firebombed in front of the rectory where it was parked. At four A.M. I was awakened by extreme heat at my bedroom window. An arsonist had poured kerosene inside and all over my car. He lit it on fire and flames exploded before my eyes. He was the same psychopath who broke into my church and desecrated the altar area and destroyed the church art and sculpture work. The man, a chemist, was eventually caught by police after committing six house deaths in the neighborhood. The man was possessed by evil and committed to a state mental institution as insane.

Another time, my face was burned while popping corn. The oil and grease exploded onto my face, and in the flames I saw a hideous, grotesque image of satan laughing at me saying, "I finally got you." I drove myself to the hospital with the stench of my burned flesh filling my nostrils. I was covered in second-degree burns and a couple areas with third-degree burns. I lost my hair, my eyebrows, my eyelashes, and my lips. The doctors were most concerned about my eyesight. They administered morphine and packed me in ice. I went into shock. For thirty straight days, the Holy Spirit visited me at my bed at the same time each morning—healing another area of my face. Each time I felt the electricity knitting together my face from all second-degree burns. After those thirty days, my face was completely restored.

Many of these spiritual attacks occurred when I had my guard down. Most occurred following a powerful experience with God. Anyone who has moved in the power of God knows it is God doing the healing work. However, He moves through us as human vessels. The anointing is awesome while it occurs. But once it lifts off, it leaves the vessel vulnerable and weak. It is my experience that it is at this time when the enemy usually attacks. Let me illustrate through an example.

One night I had just finished an event at our church where 2,000 people experienced the awesome power of God. Many were healed, delivered, and saved. My staff had all left the church for the night. I sometimes stayed at the church alone after they left to lock the building. I was rearranging chairs in the sanctuary when I heard the sound of footsteps quickly approaching me from the back of the building. As the individual came near, I wheeled around with my arms raised. Without thinking, something inside me knew the danger and spoke out, "Touch not My anointed." A man at my side trying to assault me was halted from doing so and was struck down by a supernatural power. The man was literally frozen and paralyzed at this point, as he cried out in fear the words, "Let me go; let me go!" I had him acknowledge the power of God and had him repent for his actions before I released him to move again. I had no fear. God is my Refuge and Strength.

I even remember my first, involved exorcism in New York. I was asked by a priest and leadership to lead the rite of exorcism. I agreed. When I walked into the room in street clothes to pray with the possessed person, the demons looked at me and shouted out, "We know this priest, NOT HIM." The demons know us. Many years later on the first day of work at a huge hospital as a clinical psychologist, an amazing incident happened. I was dressed in a new blue suit, looking the part of a new doctor. I walked down a corridor area, and in the hallway there was a middle-aged male patient squatting. The six new residents filed by, including me being the last in line. The male patient shouted out to me as I passed by, "We don't like priests." Demons know who we are even when we try to take on a different identity.

Many Christian churches are confused and have gross misunderstandings about teaching on demons. Most churches do not address the issue because of lack of training and knowledge. The Bible teaches, *"My people are destroyed from lack of knowledge"* (Hos. 4:6). They talk about oppression and being bothered by the demonic from the outside, but not the inside since they wrongly believe a believer who is "born again" cannot have a demon. They say a demon cannot be inside a Christian because the body is the temple of the Holy Spirit. It all sounds good; but it is wrong!

The Temple Analogy

Let me demonstrate to you from the teaching of the Word of God, the Bible. Remember, the Word is our standard of truth. If you refer to my first book, *Into His Presence,* you will discover the three separate courts to the Tabernacle of Moses, which became the pattern for building the Temple in Jerusalem. The blueprint for construction was given by God, to be followed exactly as He stated. The three courts are the Outer court, the Holy Place, and the Holy of Holies. Keep in mind that God's Word likewise states that our bodies are the temples of the Holy Spirit (see 1 Cor. 6:19). The very glory of God shines from within our temples.

Now, I would like you to think about the passage in Scripture where Jesus drives out the moneychangers in the Temple. Here we have a clear reference to deliverance. Jesus is cleansing the Temple of intruders buying and selling for profit. He says, *"My house will be a house of prayer; but you have made it a den of robbers"* (Luke 19:46). Jesus Christ is performing what I like to call Outer court ministry in my book. Demons can operate in our bodies causing physical illness and disease. This is not to say every physical disease is demonic—by no means.

The principal reason I have had so much success in praying for hundreds of individuals with cancer is that cancer is rooted in a spirit of cancer. One must take the ax to the root in order to be set free.

Also, in the Temple's outer court I teach in detail in my book *Into His Presence* about the work at the laver (basin) in the outer court. The laver is a place of washing with water. The priest would wash off the blood of the animals in the large basin just beyond the altar of sacrifice. Symbolically, it represented a place to cleanse away the residuals of sin and iniquity. It is the place symbolically where I have labored and worked as a clinical psychologist and counselor for the past thirty-plus years.

People have hurts, pain, scars, and trauma that make them vulnerable. This vulnerability and weakness allows demons to at times enter and infest a person's mind. Now remember, all of us consist of three parts—the body, the mind, and the spirit. The mind is commonly called "the soul" consisting of our thoughts, our dreams, imagination, our will, and our feelings. It is what Saint Paul calls to be renewed and transformed following the born-again experience (see Rom. 12:2).

All of this ministry symbolically takes place in the outer court of the Temple. The outer court (our body and our mind) is the place where demons victimize and lodge within. If a believer has a demon, it does not mean the believer is possessed. If someone is truly born again, the Holy Spirit has already united with the believer's spirit. The person is saved by Christ, but still struggles with issues that may be demonically rooted.

Washed in His Word of Truth

Our loving God has provided a way of healing through being washed in His Word of truth. Most of those victimized by an abuser should see satan as an abuser who comes to rob, kill, and destroy. Many people think that if demons are infesting someone's personality, that person must be evil. This is not the case. Most people I have helped over the years who have deliverance are hurting and wounded individuals who love God and want to serve God.

There are occasions, obviously, where the more heavily infested individuals do not have Christ in their lives. I am thinking about one case in which an eighteen-year-old woman came to the church prayer meeting and disrupted things by shrieking with demonic tongues. No one would go near her, they were so afraid of her. So I approached the young woman and bound the demonic so that she could speak. I then asked her what she wanted. She declared that she wanted to accept Jesus as her Savior. She confessed her sinful nature and invited Christ into her heart. I then cast out the demonic parts. She received the Baptism of the Holy Spirit in an instant and her prayer language changed dramatically from demonic to beautiful, heavenly tongues. She became a new creation in Christ.

I choose to place a heavy emphasis on the gifts of healing, faith, and miracles because Jesus placed a heavy emphasis on them. The full Gospel of Mark is characterized as a Gospel of miracles. There are nineteen miracles recorded: eight over diseases, five over the forces of nature, four over demons, and two over the power of death.

If we remove these nineteen signs and wonders plus Jesus' resurrection, there is little to nothing left in Mark's Gospel. Miracles and healing are important to Mark and to God's work among us. During His public ministry, Jesus relied on the Holy Spirit to anoint Him with power to heal. When Jesus sent out the twelve, and then the seventy-two disciples, He told them:

> *However, do not rejoice that the [evil] spirits submit to you, but rejoice that your names are written in heaven* (Luke 10:20).

The ministry of deliverance goes hand in hand with the healing ministry of the heart and soul of a person. They are both two sides of one coin and should be seen as such. I never liked being called "the Exorcist of Philadelphia." But that is in fact how some people viewed me. Some people like the idea that I played a large role as an exorcist in an unusual way. Personally, I really was never attracted to this ministry at all.

But I do realize it is a necessary ministry and part of the work of healing. I have seen, at times, the wrong people gravitate to this work. Some have a need for power and control over others. These completely lack compassion and mercy, treating the individual less like a person and more like an object. These types of people should not be in this work and ministry at all.

Above any of the gifts of the Holy Spirit in the healing ministry is the gift of discerning spirits. There are people in the ministry of healing who think everything is about demons, and there are people in the ministry of healing who think no one ever has a demon. To discern when it is appropriate to pray for deliverance is critical. Some individuals may be damaged by people in ministry who lack the gift of discernment. Some people may be left in bondage by people in ministry, who do not have the gift of discernment.

Chapter 5

A WIDER AND BROADER CHURCH

Growing up in the Roman Catholic church, we as children were indoctrinated with the idea that the Catholic church was the only true church. After all, most people in Christian circles belong to it, and we have the biggest and most beautiful cathedrals. Just look at Saint Peter's Basilica in Rome founded by the first Pope, Saint Peter, we were told. Didn't Jesus make Peter his successor? After all, Jesus said, *"And I tell you that you are Peter, and on this rock I will build my church, and the gates of Hades will not overcome it"* (Matt. 16:18).

Interestingly enough, this passage from Matthew is referring to Peter's "faith" in response to Jesus' question:

> *"Who do people say the Son of Man is?"*
> *They replied, "Some say John the Baptist; others say Elijah; and still others, Jeremiah or one of the prophets."*
> *"But what about you?" he asked. "Who do you say I am?"*
> *Simon Peter answered, "You are the Messiah, the Son of the living God."*
> *Jesus replied, "Blessed are you, Simon son of Jonah, for this was not revealed to you by flesh and blood, but by my Father in heaven"* (Matthew 16:13-17).

Because of Peter's supernatural faith (not natural), he is given a supernatural word of knowledge about the identity of Jesus. He sees Jesus as the Anointed One, the Christ, *"the Son of the living God."* It is upon this kind of "faith" that the true church would be built. It is not to be built upon Peter, a man. Then Jesus gives to Peter the keys to bind and loose the powers of darkness. I stood at the place called the "Gates of Hell or Hades" in Caesarea Philippi in Israel where Jesus spoke these words. It was a place for demonic worship and occult practices in the time of Jesus. He was telling Peter and the disciples that their faith in Him would give them power to bind and to loose demons, and that whatever demonic forces the gates of hell tried to throw at them would not prevail against them.

On a more historical point regarding apostolic succession, there is no proof that Peter even set foot in Rome from Asia Minor. He likely spent his entire ministry in Asia Minor building the early Christian community with James. There is not one shred of evidence that Peter's bones are in Rome. The Catholic church did not even form until the Age of Constantine in the fourth century. This institutionalization of Christendom actually served as the end of the times of signs and wonders because Constantine made it an edict for every citizen in the empire to be baptized as Catholic. He tried to legislate Christianity. However, we know there is only one way to God. The only way to the Father is belief in His Son Jesus as Savior and Lord. This personal relationship rejects the teaching that a person can be born into Christ by being born into an institutional organization.

NOTIONS AND ASSUMPTIONS

The notion that Peter was succeeded by an unbroken chain of popes who are infallible in their theological decrees is foolishness to anyone who is educated enough to do the research. To believe that Peter passed on these keys to Linus, Clement, Sixtus, etc. is ludicrous. The keys were passed down by the Holy Spirit for the building of the early church to those born again in the Holy Spirit. Yes, it is true that there were elders and bishops in the first three hundred years of Christianity. Leadership requires a degree of order and definition of doctrine. Hence, there is some need for overseers. There is scant to no evidence in the writings of the Fathers of the church prior to the fourth century to support the Roman Catholic claim about apostolic succession. It is weak and misleading at best.

The Book of Hebrews has impacted my life more than any other book in the Bible. Ordination as a Roman Catholic priest made me curious about the meaning of the priesthood. Did Jesus actually institute a New Testament priesthood to replace the Jewish Old Testament priesthood? In order to answer this question, we must be first familiarized with the priesthood in the Old Testament.

Deuteronomy 33:8-10 describes three essential functions of the priesthood of the Old Testament. The people of Israel went to the priest: 1) to consult God for answers to problems they had; 2) to receive teaching from the Torah or Law of God; and 3) to offer sacrifices to God for their sin. The first two duties were eventually passed on to the prophet and scribe respectively. The third duty remained the essential mark of the

Levitical priest. This third duty describes the quintessential role the Lord Jesus took on as the Lamb of God.

I say the Book of Hebrews has special significance to me because I spent eight years of my young life in preparation for ordination as a Catholic priest. I then spent nine more years as a Catholic priest in the Philadelphia area. During those years, I was influenced by a number of people. One was Martin Luther. What struck me about this forceful, historical figure was his tenacity for the truth and purity of the Word of God. I recall one Sunday morning preaching about a great saint of the church—Martin Luther. The sermon was reported to the diocese, and it served as another occasion for me to appear before chancery office authorities to answer the charges. Luther separated himself from the corruptions of the church. But he did more. Luther brought us back to the Word of God's grace by reiterating to us *"For it is by grace you have been saved, through faith—and this is not from yourselves, it is the gift of God—not by works, so that no one can boast"* (Eph. 2:8-9).

So salvation comes down to a pure gift from Jesus Christ that we either accept or reject. It is not about anything we do.

As Jesus' miraculous work grew in my ministry as a priest, more and more invitations to speak were received both within the Catholic church and outside the Catholic church. Within the Catholic church, I was receiving invitations to speak and minister healing prayer in places, parishes, and conventions throughout the Eastern Mid-Atlantic and New England states. Invitations from religious orders of nuns and priests were too numerous to mention.

"WHAT HE SAID IS TRUE"

But I must tell you about one retreat I led in Elkins Park, Pennsylvania, with 150 women. I could sense that these Catholic women were used to a nice traditional getaway for three days of peace and quiet. It was a chance for them to leave behind husbands and kids and mix in some socialization with girlfriends with some religious devotions. Little did they know that their plans were about to change. They had invited me. Simply put, although I wanted to be sensitive to their needs and routine, I wasn't one to water down the truth, especially since I was overflowing with the Spirit of the living God.

I talked to them about a personal relationship with Jesus. I laid out for them the possibility of being filled with the Holy Spirit. I even spoke on how to get prayers answered. But none of it was sinking in or making a difference in them. Finally, I wrestled with the Lord over my plight. I told Him that they didn't believe or understand a word I was saying.

He replied that my words were not going to get it done. He told me to show them with a sign and a miracle that what I was talking about is real. He told me to pick out an obvious example that all have seen and known to be real, and pray for a dramatic healing for that person. The obvious person He wanted me to choose from among all the women, was a woman hunched over severely for 17 years with degeneration of the muscle skeletal tissue. Her back was so curved that she told me she hadn't seen the ceiling of a room for 17 years.

I got very excited. God wanted to back up His Word with a miracle they could not deny. It was a beautiful Sunday morning. Sunlight filled the chapel. They were all gathered to hear another one of my sermons. This time I called the woman forward to stand beside me.

I said, "All of you know our sister, and you know her condition is irreversible. There is no medical help for her plight." I told them that over the past two days they were not buying into the Gospel I presented, although it was clearly God's Word. I told them that they seemed to prefer traditional religion and practice rather than what I came to offer them. Then I said the big, life-changing words, "That you might know that Jesus is the Son of God who heals the sick and raises the dead today, I say to this woman, 'Be loosed and set free in the name of Jesus Christ!'"

With those words, the power was released from my two hands. I never touched her directly, but directed the power over her back and spine. The healing power of God caused her vertebrae to become supple and warm. Her neck visibly straightened out and her head was upright. The crowd of women looked in astonishment as many put their hands to their faces and gasped in disbelief. Giddiness pervaded the group and a current of banter among the women. I could hear words like "What he said is true." And "Oh my God, it's a miracle" by others. The woman healed now had a smile on her face as she gazed at the chapel ceiling in awe and wonder. Wow! God backed up His Word with a sign and a miracle that Easter Sunday morning and many, many lives were altered forever!

ONCE FOR ALL

Many invitations came in from Charismatic Protestant church groups. One such group was the Full Gospel Businessmen International. I was invited to be the keynote speaker at their National Convention at the Shoreham Hotel in Washington, DC. I was enjoying breakfast with the group's president, Demos Shakarian, and several of his national leaders from 1980. They were earnest Protestant men trying to understand my Catholic approach to the Gospel.

They admitted I was a rare bird since they had never met a "saved priest" before me. I was asked numerous questions about the Mass, confession, and the Vatican. I did my very best to answer their questions. However, I could perceive that my answers were not quite hitting home for them.

In the middle of this lively discussion, an elderly woman, impeccably dressed, came over to me at the table. She excused herself for the interruption and simply looked at me saying, "I'm sorry for eavesdropping on your conversation, but the answer is in the curtain." She then disappeared as quickly as she came. To this day I believe she was an angel sent by God as a messenger for me. There is no way she was near our table because the tables were very generously spread out in this elegant dining room. The men then asked me, "What did she say to you?" I said, she simply said, "The answer is in the curtain." Demos looked over to me and said, "Go read Hebrews chapter 10."

I went up to my room and read where it is written:

> *Therefore, brothers and sisters, since we have confidence to enter into the Most Holy Place by the blood of Jesus, by a new and living way opened for us through the curtain, that is, his body...let us draw near...* (Hebrews 10:19-22).

As I read this passage, the revelation from the Spirit of God leaped off the page at me. I recalled that the curtain of the Temple was torn asunder at the very moment Jesus died on the cross. The death of Jesus made possible the dedication of the new sanctuary and opened a new and better way into the very presence of God through the veil or curtain of His flesh.

God's Holy Spirit was showing me that through Jesus, the One High Priest, all now have access to God without the need for any other intermediary. Until this time, the people needed an earthly priest to act as their intermediary between God and humanity. They needed someone to offer sin offerings to God on their behalf. I now could see clearly that Jesus came as High Priest, as the Lamb of God, as the sinless One, to end the need for any more sacrifices for sin. His death is sufficient *once for all.*

The Holy Scriptures make it evident that Jesus established through His sacrificial death on the cross a new priesthood for those who believe. He ended the need for any other sacrifice. The Catholic Mass is a sacrifice offered again and again for people's sins. Even the Catholic funeral Mass is offered in forgiveness for the deceased person's soul. It is not simply a remembrance. Any sacrifice beyond what Christ has already done is superfluous. Christ has done it all for all time. So, Jesus came not to start another priesthood of sacrifice but to end the need for one. It is finished.

Likewise, the Catholic church doctrine misinterprets the meaning of the Last Supper between Jesus and His disciples. The significance of the Passover, which He celebrated with His disciples, is that He transformed the meaning of the Passover. His words indicate that He is now the Passover meal. He became the bread broken for us and the blood poured out for us. He never intended for the gathering at the Last Supper to be a miracle of changing bread into His flesh and wine into His blood. It was a miracle of changing the meaning of the Passover!!! He gave new meaning and new significance to the Passover meal. In a few hours that same Jewish day, Jesus freely laid down His life on the cross. The day Jesus died happened to be Passover.

By speaking in conferences and meetings all across the United States, I began to see how very wide and deep is the Body of Christ's Church. The Spirit of God had me speaking to a wider audience. He spoke to me, "Carry My banner out to all nations." God was presenting a new commission.

I still believed in the need for good ministers of the Gospel. Thinking about the role of a priest acting as an intermediary to absolve sin gnawed away at me. It is taught in the Bible that no one has the power to forgive another's sin but God. When someone wrongs another, we then have the power to release them from their wrongdoing. The Word of God is clear about these things. So I had difficulty saying Mass and hearing confession ever since the Spirit of God opened my eyes to the teaching from the Book of Hebrews.

TRANSFORMATION

In 1982, having devoted just over sixteen years of my life to the priesthood, I left the role of priest in the Roman Catholic church. I visited Cardinal Archbishop to pay him the courtesy of my intent. He tried talking me out of my decision. He didn't want to lose me. But my decision was final in my mind. I obeyed the Lord, and He had bigger plans for my life.

Shortly thereafter, I was invited to the Trinity Broadcasting Network (TBN) in California. This was a television station that aired programing of charismatic interest. The television company was looking for someone to be the resident healing evangelist. It was both a national and international position. I told the producer and vice president I would think about it. At the same time, I was invited to speak with R. W. Schambach in Indianapolis and Chicago during a week-long conference and guest appearances with thousands of conference participants. God was providing open doors for me, if only I had the courage to walk through.

I didn't take advantage of these open doors that the Lord provided. I allowed shame and hurt to come rushing in upon me. Because of my obedience to leave the Catholic church, God was rewarding me. But I was too broken to accept His new invitations for ministry. I turned down both invites. Two years after I turned them down, TBN brought in Benny Hinn for the position and the network launched his worldwide healing ministry. Schambach has his own network of churches throughout the USA and was a father to many aspiring ministers. God always has a plan, and He always provides an open door when we are faithful to trust Him.

Reaction to my leaving the Catholic priesthood was serious enough among people. People were very upset. Now add to that truth the fact that I left the Catholic church, complicated people's lives all the more. I had difficulty with family and friends and all the tens of thousands of Catholic people who followed my ministry. The "Healing Priest" soon became the "Heretic Priest." People cursed me and mocked me.

People said that I was mentally ill and crazy. But I recalled they said these same things of Jesus. The Archdiocese forbad the people from attending any of my talks in Protestant churches. The Catholic newspaper published a letter warning people of my heresy. It was announced in hundreds of pulpits in the Archdiocese that I represented the worse teaching of Protestantism.

Every charismatic church group was forbidden to attend any of my talks. I suppose I should have taken these actions as compliments. The truth is the religious church saw me as a threat to lead many away from their belief system. But I must say it did hurt me to find people who once gave complete allegiance turn away from me like I had leprosy.

The gift of healing was still very active within me. The fire of God did not leave my hands. I did not leave God. I just left a denomination. Another big conference was held at Saint Mary's College in Emmitsburg, Maryland. I decided to go since the conveners were very adamant that they wanted me to come as their principal guest. The college grounds were packed with thousands of people. I called out for all eye conditions, especially cataracts, to come forward for healing prayer. Thirty-three people lined up who had cataracts and in an instant one after another were healed by divine surgery as I laid my hands on their eyes. This was amazing! All praise be to God. It was such an unbelievable occurrence that the newspaper in York, Pennsylvania, published news about the thirty-three miracles. It was also a confidence builder for me that the Holy Spirit had not taken away my gift because I left the Roman Catholic church and disappointed people.

ANOTHER PURSUIT

But my sensitivities run very deep. I had difficulty warding off the voices of condemnation from the Catholic church. So because of my personal inner wounds from the voices and former friends, I made a questionable decision. I thought, *Who needs this hassle of ministry. I don't need the pain it brings anymore.* I left my heart and went into my head again. It has always been comfortable to live in my intellect. After all, I had been accepted into MENSA, an organization for high IQ people, at seventeen years of age.

So I went back to pursuing a doctorate in clinical psychology at the University of Maryland. I visited the school in the summer when I had moved to Baltimore, Maryland. I was given an interview with the chairperson of the department of psychology and the dean of the clinical program. They looked at my SAT and GRE scores and college transcripts and accepted me on the spot before I applied to the school. How ridiculously backward this procedure was! Who in the world gets accepted to a university before even applying to the university? Then who doesn't have to wait for another year before starting the semester? Only God could do such a miracle! I started in September with only three other doctoral students accepted. God was still taking care of me in spite of myself.

Perhaps the Holy Spirit had another plan for my life. I certainly won supernatural favor at this prestigious school program. God's hand was on my life even when I thought I had passed up other opportunities. I was still His beloved son who needed a long rest from all the chaos and warfare.

In pursuing doctoral level psychology, I found my spiritual beliefs quickly tested. There were no other Christians in my circles. Everyone was either an agnostic or an atheist. I convinced myself that my belief and faith were strong enough to withstand humanism. It became a real battle. God carefully warns about mixing the things above with the things below. He says, *"Be careful not to make a treaty with those who live in the land where you are going, or they will be a snare among you. Break down their altars, smash their sacred stones and cut down their Asherah poles"* (Ex. 34:12-13).

Passing into a passionate relationship with Jesus requires that we keep our focus on Him. When we take our eyes off of Him, we are bound to fall. But my head began to be filled with secular knowledge. This direction was to be my course and pattern.

Chapter 6

THE PRODIGAL RETURNS

The story of Joseph in the Old Testament tells of a man who was able to keep his heart right before God. In spite of his circumstances, he did not harden his heart against his brothers who betrayed him or against the Lord who allowed his brothers to mistreat, abuse, abandon, and leave for dead in a pit in the ground.

Joseph kept his eyes upon God and believed in God's greater sovereignty over his life rather than believing in the power that sin and jealousy to ruin his life. It is an incredible grace to live this way! Joseph still believed God was in control, and because he believed his purpose was in God's hands, he knew he was right where God wanted him to be.

Sometimes we think we know what is best for us. Sometimes we think we know how things should work out. When things don't go the way expected, we can become disturbed and angry. At times we might even get angry with God. This was my unfortunate reaction to hurt and rejection. I am not proud of it, but I need to tell you the bad as well as the good. The Lord and I had walked in an incredible relationship of love and intimacy. He was my best Friend. I thought our friendship was unbreakable.

But following the pain and hurt of rejection and abandonment by close friends and the Catholic church at large, I found myself living in my car with eight cents in my pocket. I had no place to live and no one to turn to for help. I felt like an outcast. Although I had been accepted for graduate studies, I had no money, no credit, and no benefactors. I was now in a different state, in Maryland, where I had no friends or contacts. My salary as a Catholic priest was at the time $4,000 annually plus some stipend money. For eight days I lived out of my car, and washed up in a gas station in Baltimore. I wondered how things could have turned on me so quickly.

Even more telling for me was the thought that my best Friend, the Lord, could allow people to hurt me so badly when all I wanted to do was to heal people in His name? I was naïve enough to believe everyone would welcome healing. This was far from the truth. I had to fight with the authorities of the church for years; I had to be dragged before religious judges for years; I had to curb and curtail my healing services and answer to legalistic laws that modified the healing meetings; and I had to answer to the Cardinal Archbishop for praying for the healing of a woman at a Sunday Mass who was cured of a back condition.

All of these nagging attacks mounted up over time and wore me down. It is the random, repeated, picking and prodding and pulling that can eventually defeat someone's optimism and break the person's spirit. The spiritual attacks came in the form of being ostracized in a rectory for three years. No clergy ate meals with me because of my beliefs. Covertly, two priests tried to frame me with untruths to destroy my reputation. They were unsuccessful, and God had the final word on His priestly son with the chancery office.

Interestingly enough, the attacks almost always were from within the religious system, and not from outside the religion. In Jesus' time, the same thing occurred. The attacks always arose from within the religious establishment including scribes, Pharisees, and Sanhedrin.

God designed my personality to have a great capacity for intensity to feel things deeply. This sensitivity can be used for better or for worse. Psalm 55:12-14 expresses what it feels like to be hurt by someone close to us:

> *If an enemy were insulting me, I could endure it; if a foe were rising against me, I could hide. But it is you, a man like myself, my companion, my close friend, with whom I once enjoyed sweet fellowship at the house of God, as we walked about among the worshipers.*

The pain of betrayal runs deep. When best friends turn their backs on you, and you have no friend to turn to, it can be devastating enough. But when, with clouded vision, you perceive God betraying you, it can seem like an incurable wound. Jeremiah must have felt this way when he wrote:

> *I had been like a gentle lamb led to the slaughter. I did not realize that they had plotted against me, saying, "Let us destroy the tree and its fruit; let us cut him off from the land of the living, that his name be remembered no more"* (Jeremiah 11:19).

I found myself saying with Jeremiah: *"O Lord, You duped me, and I let myself be duped"* (Jer. 20:7). It is easy to do what I did and turn away from God in this time of trial. At times like these it is very difficult to dwell on the promises of God, which sound so farfetched.

> *Everyone who has left houses or brothers or sisters or father or mother or wife or children or fields for my sake will receive a hundred times as much and will inherit eternal life* (Matthew 19:29).

The truth of these words notwithstanding, I did leave my God behind. Joseph knew betrayal too; he was sold as a slave; he endured ten years in a prison cell. But he never gave up on his God. Through trial and pain he kept close to the Lord. He never asked "Why me, Lord!" He never blamed God. I did all the above. Joseph was given two sons. The first he called Manasseh, the second he named Ephraim.

> *Joseph named his firstborn Manasseh and said, "It is because God has made me forget all my trouble and all my father's household." The second son he named Ephraim and said, "It is because God has made me fruitful in the land of my suffering"* (Genesis 41:51-52).

The land of Joseph's suffering was Egypt where Joseph was appointed by Pharaoh to take charge over the whole land of Egypt. He was in charge of all the grain at the time of a great famine in the land. God blessed His son's victory over evil done against him. God blessed him in a land ruled by God's enemy.

WALKING AWAY

I was not as wise as Joseph. I recall at the time saying, "I will never allow myself to be hurt ever again." I figuratively left my open heart to live from that day forward in my head. I would not allow feelings to get in the way again. Unfortunately, when we do this, we close off the possibilities of love and friendship. All personal relationship and risk is taken off the table. To love means by its very nature to be vulnerable. Love opens us up to the possibility of being hurt with emotional pain. We can't have one without the other. That is the package deal. That is the way it works.

Please understand me that going on to school for higher education is not a bad thing. It was detrimental for me because I stepped out of my calling to be a minister. Yet God can redeem all of our choices and decisions. He can take something and turn it for our good. When I chose to lean upon my own understanding rather than God's understanding, I noticed more and more a falling away from God. I stopped praying to Him. I stopped talking to Him. I no longer went to church, and I preached less and less at churches. This was a process that crept in like a flood. Before I knew it, I was no different from the people I was around in academia. The Word of God says:

> *Trust in the Lord with all your heart and lean not on your own understanding; in all your ways submit to him, and he will make your paths straight* (Proverbs 3:5-6).

My God never failed me. He never gave up on me. He used the story of the prodigal son, or the lost son, to lure me back home to Him. It was not until many years later that I realized how bad things had become for me. Sure, I was a board certified clinical psychologist with a great job and a beautiful wife. But I had changed. And the change was not for the better but for the worse. I was now worshipping at the doorstep of the intellect. My colleagues and friends called me jokingly "Dr. Sigmund Freud Sizer."

I didn't pray. I was glad most of those years not to be bothered with God. Imagine this! One who walked so intimately with the Lord, now didn't even consider Him. One who saw miraculous accounts done by His hand, now forgot about all that in favor of secular humanism and cognitive behavioral therapy. Wow— this seems inconceivable to me even as I write this. So, how did the journey back home happen? I will begin to tell you through the parable.

> *Jesus continued: "There was a man who had two sons. The younger one said to his father, 'Father, give me my share of the estate.' So he divided his property between them. Not long after that, the younger son got together all he had, set off for a distant country and there squandered his wealth in wild living. After he had spent everything, there was a severe famine in that whole country, and he began to be in need"* (Luke 15:11-14).

Thank God for the place of need. It is only when we find ourselves at a place of need that we can be saved. Without a need, we are self-sufficient. Faced with trial and troubles bigger than ourselves, we can at least have the possibility to turn to someone else for help. A place of need puts us in touch with our mistakes and sin. This is what happens to the lost son who wandered off to a place he didn't belong. The words "distant country" are both literal and symbolic words. It is a place where you shouldn't be because it represents a false nature of who you are. Jesus goes on to say:

> *"When he came to his senses, he said, 'How many of my father's hired servants have food to spare, and here I am starving to death! I*

> *will set out and go back to my father and*
> *say to him: Father, I have sinned against*
> *heaven and against you. I am no longer*
> *worthy to be called your son; make me like*
> *one of your hired servants.' So he got up and*
> *went to his father..."* (Luke 15:17-20).

When the son *"came to his senses"* indicates an awakening and realization that he had it better back at his father's house than where he was now. Yes, it does hurt at times to love others, but it hurts more not to love at all. Like the prodigal son, I realized and became aware that I was a happier, better person with the Lord than without the Lord. I now knew that I needed to repent of my sins, renounce the curses I put on my life, and return to God.

WALKING HOME

I got reacquainted with God following the birth of my newborn son. God showed me love again. I felt safe expressing love to my little son. God knew the little child would be a safe place for my wounded heart to express itself. I remember sitting on the floor before my child in his carrier. In an instant, without ever thinking it through, I transferred all the love I had for my son into a scene in which God my Father took over my place as Daddy to my son, and I took over my son's place as a tiny child. This spontaneous therapy was incredible as tears flooded my soul. His love for me was overwhelming! Our relationship was being restored.

This is the reaction we see from the father toward his lost son.

> "...But while he was still a long way off, his father saw him and was filled with compassion for him; he ran to his son, threw his arms around him and kissed him" (Luke 15:20).

The father's reaction is one of love for his son who has returned home. The father doesn't demand an explanation for his son's behavior. The father doesn't say, "I told you so." He simply embraces his son with open arms and welcomes him back home. This Gospel story is the perennial story of a loving father waiting for the return of his wayward children with open arms. It sums up the one vital message I believe God wants to communicate to us through the pages of the Bible, namely, "I Love You."

How utterly ridiculous for us ever to think that our faith consists in what we can do for God. Our faith is in fact totally based on what God does for us. Our faith is not about keeping laws so that we can be nicer people with nicer morals. This would be an insult to God, and tantamount to a prostitution of the good news.

The staggering truth of the matter is that God does not love us in some vague, philosophical way. He doesn't love us in some esoteric way. Nothing could be further from the truth. GOD IS LOVE. He can do nothing but love by nature. Intrinsically and extrinsically GOD IS LOVE. The proof of this love is that He died in our place so that we may be with Him forever.

Like thousands of people before me, He saw that I wasn't beyond help. He waited for me to take that first step back toward Him, then pounced on that very first opportunity to pour out His love. He told me that day with my newborn son, "For all these years I waited for you, Frank. You who ran from Me, and didn't want to hear My name ever again. When I lost you, Frank, I lost My best friend." These words from God Almighty were almost too much for me to take in.

I thought who in this world could ever love me as much as He loves me? His love is forever and it is real, oh so real. I then said to Him, "Lord, let me never leave You again. For my life has no meaning; it makes no sense; it has no purpose if You are not at the center of my existence."

CRAZY IN LOVE

God is crazy in love with you, too. He does not condemn you or judge you. We do a pretty good job of that to ourselves. And others in our life do a pretty good job of managing to criticize us. Judgment is made by our own choices and by the world's choices. God's Word teaches that God even loves those who hate Him. The Son reigns on the just and on the unjust. So, God's love is so insanely generous that He not only loves those who embrace Him by name but also loves those who would reject Him by name.

Somehow in our weak, unbiblical thinking, we conspire to make God as someone distant, or someone detached from us—when He actually knows every hair on our head. We mistakenly come to believe that we have to earn His approval like we earn a teacher's approval. If we act proper and good, then He will love us. We learn He simply accepts us as we are. He forgives and forgets our indiscretions. His way is pure amnesty. His love for us is based on nothing that comes from us. It is all based on the fact that we are His creations and belong by nature to Him.

The old vindictive images we have of God need to give way to the truth about love and mercy. God cherishes you like no one else. God loves you like no one else. God wants relationship with you like no one else. In spite of your reluctance and reticence, He still chooses to forgive you and bless you. He liberates from deserved punishment; He forgets all abuse toward Him; and He calls you to a life of forever love.

Chapter 7

POWER THAT RELEASES WISDOM

T he road back to a life with God had a direct effect on my attitude toward psychology. Like so many others before me who studied psychology in detail, I succumbed to it like a god. It provided an understanding of human behavior backed up by robust studies substantiating the behavior patterns and outcomes. I enjoyed delving into personality theories, interpersonal interactions, and communication protocol. Beyond this were cognitive techniques and neuroscience I would have never understood had I not studied and learned them.

However, by regaining my relationship with God, I had to submit my intellectual knowledge of psychology to the Lord. I asked the Holy Spirit to wash away all the rift and dross from graduate school that was useless, and help me to retain what was useful. All that remained, I submitted to the Lord. This process gave supremacy unto the Lord once more.

Over time, the Holy Spirit has helped me to develop a private practice that integrates my knowledge of people—including personality development, mental illness, and cognition, and affect—with the power of healing the mind through prayer guided by the Holy Spirit and the Word of God! The knowledge of psychology is subordinated to the primacy of Holy Spirit. The consequences of this integration yield no conflict between God's truth and God's Word and knowledge of human behavior.

One very basic truth regained is the truth that ever since the Fall of Adam at the beginning of humanity, sin has contaminated every person. No one can escape it. Original sin affects heredity, genetics, biology, and our environment.

No child enters this world as a proverbial "blank slate" as some used to teach. The notion that everything is learned is false and deceptive. We all enter life with predispositions to certain diseases, as well as particular psychological traits and dispositions. As God's

Word teaches us, we are all marked by original sin. This means that as beautiful as a newborn baby may be, the child is already genetically tainted by original sin. There are several references in the Word of God to this truth, among them the following:

> *Surely I was sinful at birth, sinful from the time my mother conceived me* (Psalm 51:5).

In the same psalm, God indicates that we are affected by both sin and iniquity, or curses, when He says:

> *Wash away all my iniquity and cleanse me from my sin* (Psalm 51:2).

Sin is not a very popular subject for discussion in society, and even in many churches it is avoided at the pulpit in favor of positive thinking. As believers, we thank God for the gift of grace abounding toward us, yet we must also be aware of our faults and frailties impeding our relationships. Our personal sin and foibles cannot be overlooked. Also, our culture has embraced a philosophy of situation ethics that helps in denial of taking personal responsibility for one's behavior and whitewashing any wrongdoing. Many people believe that if it feels right then do it, as long as they believe it doesn't hurt or harm anyone else. We live in an age of tolerance and political correctness. The consequences of this kind of approach to morality leads to a tolerance of sin.

Sin becomes so much a part of our fabric of society that we don't even recognize it as sin anymore. The result left behind is that believers don't seem to be too much different from nonbelievers in their behaviors. Faith becomes relegated to church practice on Sunday. The rest of the week our behavior looks very secular and much the same as anybody else's behavior. Ever since Cain killed his brother Abel, the battle of sin has raged on earth. Jeremiah the prophet says, *"The heart is deceitful above all things"* (Jer. 17:9). Becoming aware of our own sin and shortcomings is actually a gift whereby we can seek forgiveness and change. Such awareness can lead us on the path of closeness with God.

NARCISSISM

In Greek mythology, there is a story of a young handsome youth who looks into a pond of water and sees his reflection and falls in love with himself. He can't take his eyes off himself and literally falls into the water and drowns. It is the story of how narcissism develops. It is a character disorder of self-absorption that puts the highest priority on one's selfish nature. A person with this mental disorder lives with a pervasive pattern of grandiosity, a lack of empathy, and a hypersensitivity to criticism and the evaluation of others.

Narcissism is a stage in early childhood development that most people manage to break through and beyond. As a child recognizes that he or she is not the center of the universe, it is a rude and jolting wake-up call. However, most children come to adapt to this reality of life. We have all either heard of or have navigated a child through the "terrible twos." The child's temper flares and the child wants what it wants. Giving in to the child most of the time only reinforces the behavior. The selfish nature becomes engrained. The narcissistic child is then wed "to the selfish creature" for identity rather than reaching out toward others and ultimately God. There is little to no chance for altruism and generosity to develop in this person.

Some Christians can be naïve enough to believe that once they are saved in Christ, every weakness and flaw disappears from their lives. The truth is that we are all called to grow up. We need to be patient with our selfish nature and see God work with us to break our patterns of selfishness as we become more like Him. Sanctification and transformation are a process over time. The change will come eventually through the grace and work of the Holy Spirit.

Unhealthy Shame

Another condition which besets many is the feeling of unhealthy shame. When Adam and Eve walked with God in The Garden, they were not ashamed (Gen. 2:25). The result of the Fall plunged them into the human condition of shame to the extent that they covered themselves. Sin brings on shame (Gen. 3:10).

A common way to deal with shame is to cover it up in deception. We commonly do it by presenting ourselves as persons whom we are really not. Shame brings on a false sense of self. We end up covering our true selves with a false portrayal of who we really are. And in our wounded nature we then seek to "fit in" through things that will never lead us to wholeness—things like alcohol, drugs, sex addiction, promiscuity, adultery, and the like. Our false image leads us further away from our true selves and from God Himself.

For more than 30 years, I have professionally worked as a board certified clinical psychologist with thousands of patient hours to my practice. Many present as simply persons struggling for acceptance and peace of mind. Many are abused; most are wounded. Their thoughts and feelings are clouded by past memories of individuals, many times significant individuals like parents and spouses, who have hurt them and damaged them to a point whereby it is damaging. In other cases, they are the ones who have done the damage and need to make amends. Sometimes we find ourselves dealing with deep-seated self-hatred and perhaps hatred of God for thinking that He was not there to protect them.

Our tragedies and disappointments need to be addressed and ultimately viewed from a divine perspective. This point will only be arrived at through an honesty and a willingness to face the real feelings. Uncovering ourselves before a nonjudgmental therapist is usually vital in leading us back to a loving God. The walls of protection, which have built up over the years of keeping others at a distance, need to come down. Feelings of love and intimacy come with trust reborn. Mere survival can transform into living in abundance.

No Longer Victims

The beauty and reward in this work is to eventually see victims no longer acting like victims. They no longer define themselves by a sin, by a drug, or by hurts and pains from their past. They see the cross of Jesus in all its power disarm every demon power in hell. He takes away their former authority, He uncovers their crafty deceptive lies, and He gives back the power and authority to the victim–patient.

The pathogenic relationship to a false identity gives way to wholeness and healing in Jesus. Issues of abandonment, rejection, insecurity, depression, and anxiety are now washed in the truth of Christ's love for them.

There is something I need to say to churches, pastors, and people who seek out prayer support and counseling in churches. Occasionally there are found pastors with professional credentials to practice counseling. However, many pastors are by and large naïve when dealing with people having problems who seek out help in their church. People with serious issues often go to a pastor or lay leader for help. There are many pastors and church leaders who take on situations that really require professional help and assistance. It is vital for church leadership to know when to refer someone with a problem beyond their purview to a good professional health care provider.

Without the proper training and credentials, significant harm may be done to individuals who trust their church. Giving advice, counseling, and deeper therapeutic inner healing are in the wheelhouse and purview of those professionally trained and experienced in such methods. In my own years of witnessing what damage can occur in some churches, it is alarming and frightening. Even when lay counselors for churches have a semblance of what to say and how to direct people, there is still the likelihood of confidentialities being broken and people's personal lives being made public through broken confidences.

I have worked with good pastors who refer their people to me. The relationship of trust is already

established because they know me. They are nonintru-
sive and do not interfere with the counseling process.
They are wise enough to know their own limitations as
pastors and do not try to be counselors. They see their
role as sharing the Gospel as pastors and do not put on
another hat to be a counselor. If they have prayer teams
in their church, they make sure their teams bring prayer
and not counseling. Their teams advise people when to
seek further professional help for their individual problems. This wise process keeps liability issues for the
church at bay, and it also keeps the lines and boundar-
ies of what the church is to accomplish in check. These
are important guidelines for any church to follow if
they desire to be in the will of God.

We might say that Jesus Himself is the master psychologist. He knew how to talk to people. In the Gospel
of Saint John, Jesus encounters a Samaritan woman at
the well. Here we have a beautiful story of Jesus taking
the time to speak with a woman who was living out of
a false sense of self. We don't know much about her his-
tory, nor her family, but we can say that she struggled
with a deep sense of shame.

She came to the well at a time when other women
would not be there. Twice a day early in the morning
and evening the other women would come to the well.
This woman came at noon in order to avoid them. Jesus

speaks words to her that manage to turn her attention away from the well water to something deeper. He says:

"If you knew the gift of God and who it is that asks you for a drink, you would have asked him and he would have given you living water" (John 4:10).

Jesus is asking her to surrender her entire self over to Him. He wants to change her and give her a water that will fill her with new life. He gently disposes her to receive Him. This is generally how He transforms each person He meets. His goal is to get the woman to gaze into the deepest well of eternal love. This is the place where she will be transformed. In the amazement of endless love, the woman will give up her false self with all her defense mechanisms keeping people out.

Her desire to fulfill love and needs in all the wrong places with all the wrong things, will now give way to something real and lasting. Her repetitious thirst drove her to fill her needs with natural appetites and tendencies again and again. She compulsively and obsessively tried to fill her wounded soul. Jesus deftly calls her out of shame by graciously exposing her places of shame. Watch what He says to her:

"Go, call your husband and come back." "I have no husband," she replied. Jesus said to her, "You are right when you say you have

> *no husband. The fact is, you have had five*
> *husbands, and the man you now have is not*
> *your husband..."* (John 4:16-17).

The fear of being exposed is what lies in the pit of shame. Jesus knew that she hid this truth in shame. But He gently uncovers it realizing her vulnerability. The master psychotherapist enters into a place heretofore forbidden to anyone. Shame holds the woman back from intimacy with God. It keeps her at a distance.

Fear cripples, on the other hand. It causes one to lie about the truth. When love shows up, it disarms all condemnation. The gentle reminder of truth by Jesus in His word of knowledge stirs in her little threat. *"A bruised reed he will not break, and a smoldering wick he will not snuff out..."* (Isa. 42:3).

By reminding the woman of her five marriages and her current affair, Jesus has led her to a place of conviction and repentance. She accepts His gift of forgiveness and love. The woman's shame is removed. It is the essential component to her testimony. In its place she receives "living water." The very story she once so carefully kept hidden, she now shouts out loud because Jesus has set her free!

> *Then, leaving her water jar behind, the*
> *woman went back to the town and said*
> *to the people, "Come, see a man who told*

me everything I ever did. Could this be the Messiah?" (John 4:28-29)

Putting down the water jar and leaving it behind meant putting down her former life. The woman now had much more important things to talk about. She hurries back to the people she once avoided. She is now dressed in a mantle of love and confidence coming from God. The living water bubbles up within her and out of her. Once of ill repute, she is changed and alive through the presence and healing words of Jesus. This is what real therapy is like. This is what real therapy can do.

Broken People Transformed

Like the story of the Samaritan woman at the well, the Bible is full of examples of broken persons transformed by the hand of mercy and love. God touches the sinner, the broken, the lost, the abandoned, and the rejected. The account of Samuel the prophet going to the house of Jesse to anoint a new king for Israel is a case in point. Jesse lines up seven sons for the prophet's inspection. But the prophet is told by the Spirit of God that none of them is the one. He says to Jesse, "Don't you have any more sons?" Jesse replied I have one tending the sheep. He was brought to the house, and God told Samuel:

> *"...Rise and anoint him; this is the one." So Samuel took the horn of oil and anointed*

him in the presence of his brothers, and
from that day on the Spirit of the Lord
came powerfully upon David..." (1 Samuel
16:12-13).

In the story, David wasn't even included with his
seven brothers by his own father. Many in families and
society know what it is like to be marginalized or not
counted. It is a lonely and isolating feeling. Rejection
can be a common experience. David certainly knew
the experience. Yet it really doesn't matter whether
you were rejected or abandoned. God provides in His
loving-kindness.

It is interesting that the very thing we didn't have
in life from our family, friends, or community is the
very thing that drives us into the arms of God's love.
We cannot come to God in success and greatness and
power. We can only come to God in weakness and vulnerability. We come to God like a child in need. We
kneel before Him; He anoints us; and we arise as a king
or a queen. He not only cancels our former life and
ways of sin, but also restores us above and beyond.

Our salvation in Christ gives us a new identity. Our
mind is now on a path of transformation. With Saint
Paul, we understand when he writes:

You were taught, with regard to your former
way of life, to put off your old self, which

is being corrupted by its deceitful desires; to be made new in the attitude of your minds; and to put on the new self, created to be like God in true righteousness and holiness (Ephesians 4:22-24).

God's desire is to reclaim each one of us by allowing us to die to our old, false selves. He then leads us to be born again into a new self, made in His image and likeness. It should be noted that when Jesus was crucified on the cross, He was pierced in His side by a soldier's lance. Blood and water flowed from His side. The blood releases us from guilt, but the water frees us from shame. Both the sin of guilt and the iniquity of shame are removed by Christ on the cross. Good psychotherapist knows how to apply the work of Christ here, and to lead a person into restoration.

Chapter 8

POWER-RELEASING
REVIVAL

I had been back to going to church since the birth of my son in 1990, yet at this time in 1994 I was still reticent to minister and to take back my position in apostolic ministry. I was then reminded in Scripture about the verse when God gives a gift He does not withhold it. The Word of God teaches that,

> *...for God's gifts and his call are irrevocable* (Romans 11:29).

The call and gift of apostleship was resident in me, but only like an ember of fire barely burning inside.

The fire within was hardly noticeable to me since it had not been used for a number of years. My hands that were once on fire and always warm to hot didn't emanate a tangible anointing. It was no wonder I had no visible sign of the gift of miracles. After all, my identity was currently as a doctor of psychology, not an ordained minister. The other decisive reality was that I had walked away from a life moving in miracles and told God I didn't want any part of it anymore. In my mind He didn't protect me enough, so why stick my neck out for Him.

The Word of God encourages us to fan into flame the gift of God. Without the rekindling, it is almost useless. What I didn't know was that another rebirth was about to take place in me. The flame was about to burn, burn, burn.

LOVE AND MERCY

In January 1994, the first outbreak of revival occurred in Toronto, Canada, since the Charismatic Renewal in the 1970s. Millions flocked to Toronto to experience a newfound love from the heavenly Father. Many were brought to God through the Father's love. The experience produced a tangible presence of God like entering into the Holy of Holies in the Tabernacle of the Old Testament. The revival experience was transported from Canada to Great Britain and then to Pensacola, Florida. Curious as I am, I took a trip in 1994 to Toronto to see for myself what was going on.

I walked into the conference auditorium. There were more than 5,000 people in attendance. During the time for personal prayer, teams of leaders were stationed throughout the hall. As prayer for an impartation of the Holy Spirit was given by the teams, people were falling down like flies under the power of God. The anointing was strong and heavy. Many were shaking. I looked up as if to God and said, "You're back, Lord." The manifest presence of God brings His power that can cause a shaking. God's Word says:

> "...*Once more I will shake not only the earth but also the heavens." The words "once more" indicate the removing of what can be shaken—that is, created things—so that what cannot be shaken may remain* (Hebrews 12:26-27).

God was shaking off the sin and dross of the flesh. He was allowing only the things of His nature to remain. At this point, a pastor friend intervened for me. He approached the conference speaker to have him pray for me. As he prayed for me he smiled since my friend told him I was a Catholic priest with a great healing ministry during the Charismatic Renewal.

He gently laid hands on me and I fell to the ground under the weight of the anointing. I shook again on the floor and felt the love of God upon me. My stomach began to contort. I coughed a few times. I was on the floor for a good while; the coughing gave way to tears, and a release of joy ensued thereafter. I experienced a deliverance. Many times, deliverance is accompanied by belching, coughing, or vomiting. In this case it was connected to aspects of a hurting and an unforgiving heart. My heart was healed again by the love of the Father.

The conference was all about the heavenly Father's love and mercy. I was so touched by the experience of it all that I recall breaking into laughter. Not that there was anything funny about what just occurred in me, but holy laughter welled up from inside like a spring of water. This truth and now reality played right into my need. It reminded me of the Scripture where it is written:

> *Isaac reopened the wells that had been dug in the time of his father Abraham, which the Philistines had stopped up after Abraham died...* (Genesis 26:18).

The beautiful wells dug by Abraham led to life for the Israelites for many years. Then the enemy came in and occupied the land. They stopped up the wells by filling them in with dirt. This is to say that God in

His sovereign nature dug a deep spiritual well inside me. For years and years, it brought forth miraculous signs and wonders, giving drink and life to whomever I would minister.

FRESH WATER REBIRTH

Then with the hurt and with the pain that ensued, I turned away from God and I turned away from the apostolic ministry. The enemy came and filled in the well with demonic thoughts and attitudes. I replaced my first love with a false idol. But thank God, He never gives up on us. That day in Toronto He reclaimed His son's call and gift as an apostle. God reopened the well and new, fresh water poured on out. My ministry was reborn.

Calls for ministry to churches and calls to speak at national and international conferences came flooding in following the reinstatement. This is proof that all God is looking for is a willing servant and an open heart. As a matter of fact, I ministered at that very church in Toronto for an entire week. My wife and son joined me in praying with people from many different nations—from Germany to Finland to Ireland and the United Kingdom all gathered around the same altar.

My son Joshua, who was six years of age at the time, spoke with a man who had wandered in the first night.

He happened to be despondent and depressed, and was going to take his life, but found himself in the church around the altar for prayer. The man tested the Lord and said, "Give me a reason for not taking my life when I am prayed over." My little son happened along. He laid his hands over the man and prayed out loud for him. The man was so touched by the prayer that he wept and cried; touched by the loving prayer of the child. The following day the man brought his wife and children to meet my son, and to give thanks to the Lord for saving his life.

In 1996, I led a revival that broke out in Cleveland, Ohio. It covered the entire Cleveland region near where I lived at the time. People gathered five nights a week for ten months straight. Every night Monday through Friday in excess of 350 people came.

The most striking thing about the revival was that intercessors would find themselves praying for hours before services. Mostly women, these intercessors produced an awesome army of prayer warriors. The presence of God was thick and tangible every night.

Healings, miracles, and families coming to the Lord abounded. Some nights we could see what looked like a cloud thickening over the church sanctuary. In the Old Testament this thick cloud is referred to as the *kabod,* or glory of the Lord. When the glory came, our shoes were taken off for we knew it was holy ground.

Just as Moses took off his shoes when God appeared in the burning bush, so did we do the same. This presence lent the moment to silence and to bowing before Him.

The word *kabod* means weight, so all things bow to the heaviness of the glory presence. On more than one occasion, the weight of God's glory caused me to collapse to the ground. My words would not form on my lips, my brain felt inoperable, and there was no preaching on those nights. The cloud of God's glory was directly related to the women's prayer and praises. God Himself loved it. He presented Himself more and more as He heard the women's praises.

FOR THE LOVE OF CHILDREN

Some of the most beautiful experiences was seeing teenagers and children in awe at the Presence of God. Tears of joy filled the faces of boys and girls.

Speaking of children, I recall ministering in a large Houston, Texas, church where I was preaching at two morning services. Between the services, the church provided a guest room for relaxing. A six-year-old girl brought her ten-year-old sister who was born "deaf and dumb" to the room. She asked me to pray for her older sister as they held hands. She specifically asked me to ask Jesus to heal her sister so she could hear and talk.

How could Jesus refuse. I cast out the deaf spirit and then the dumb spirit in Jesus' name. I then clicked my fingers to see that she could hear. A big smile broke out on her little face and she nodded in the affirmative. I then asked her to look at my lips, and I had her pronounce her first word. I told her to say the word, "Jesus." The two syllables came forth one at a time. "Je" "sus"; then finally "Jesus." We broke into applause at what the good Lord had done. I then introduced the two girls at the beginning of the second service so the entire church community could thank God that Sunday morning! This was the third time I had seen Jesus heal a person from a deaf and dumb spirit.

When I returned to ministry, one of my first meetings was held in Nashville, Tennessee. During the time of ministry, I pointed out in the audience a fifteen-year-old girl standing to my left. She had a huge goiter growing on the left side of her neck. I spoke that the Spirit of the Lord said she was being healed right now. The power of these words caused her to crash to the floor. Metal chairs fell along with her. I then walked over to her and placed my hand on her neck.

Immediately the tumor went down, down, and then was gone. Her father stood over her crying at what the Lord had done. He had hearing aids in each ear. He told me artillery fire damaged her ears while serving in the military. I told him to take out of his ears the two hearing aids. I prayed, and God instantly opened both ears, healing his punctured eardrums.

While these two miracles were going on, a pretty little three-year-old girl was twirling around beside her mother in the back of the auditorium. The little girl tugged on her mommy and shouted in excitement to her, "Mommy, Mommy, look at the man up front." The mother said, "Yes, that is Dr. Sizer, the preacher." But the little girl replied, "No, not him. I mean the beautiful man behind him." The little child saw a beautiful big angel standing behind me as I ministered in signs and wonders like I had done so very many times in the 1970s and 1980s. God was reaffirming to me the ministry of miracles that He had imparted upon me many years before. He was confirming His great works through the archangel's presence ministering with me. This was thrilling news to me.

A Special Angel

In 1975, the Spirit of God had told me that He would send a special angel with me to heal the sick. He further told me the name of the angel. He said the name of the angel that would accompany me is "Raphael." I didn't think much about Raphael's name until some years later. The Hebrew prefix "rapha" means "Healing" and the suffix "el" means God. His name means, "I Am the God Who Healeth Thee." The Bible teaches that God uses angels to minister healing in the name of the Lord Jesus. Raphael specifically is found in deutero-canonical Scriptures as the "Healing Angel."

It is my hope and prayer that as you get hold of this message you will come to understand that an entire world exists in another dimension that most cannot see. When we enter into this realm or dimension, our eyesight changes from glory to glory.

We can perceive that the invisible is more real than the visible. We come to see the unseen as more real than the sensate. This kind of perception opens one up to the "things of the Spirit realm." The angels we sometimes talk about at the portal of glory are now willing vessels guarding and watching over our very lives.

I never would want to presume on God's goodness, so my approach toward ministry was to try to keep humble. I made sure that I would give Him the glory for whatever signs and wonders occurred. When moving in ministry, I did not presume the angel walked beside me; if he did then so be it. One thing I do know is that we cannot control the Spirit of God showing up in a service. We pray that the Lord would be gracious toward us and bless us as we give our very best to Him.

SUPERNATURAL GIFTS

Moving in supernatural gifts is no doubt very exciting. The gift of word of knowledge is one of the wisdom gifts of the Holy Spirit. You can read about it in First Corinthians, chapter 12. When I point out someone, a strong sense of knowing something supernatural comes over me. I know things that I shouldn't know. Let me give you a few examples of moving in the gift of word of knowledge.

Shortly before this meeting in Indiana, I was ministering in Minnesota where I walked over to a man I had never met before. I looked at him and told him that his gift was wisdom from God. I said he would guide and direct many people in Christian counseling. It turned out he was a licensed counselor.

At a meeting in southern New Jersey, I walked over to a man and said, "You are a boat captain and fish for a living. Now you, like Peter, will become a fisher of men." His name was Bob Bradbury. He went into ministry having dropped his captain's nets. He helped evangelize young people in the country of Uraguay for a number of years thereafter.

Recently, I mentioned to a small group of forty people in Pennsylvania that a woman present in the room is a fraternal twin. The Spirit of God told me that she had a falling out with her sister two months before, so I said that out loud. God wanted her to step forward for prayer now and reconcile with her sister who wronged her. A woman stepped forward and declared it was her. She asked the Lord Jesus for forgiveness on the spot. Chances of a fraternal twin in a group of forty people is low odds if one was guessing. It is easy to say such a thing to a crowd of five thousand but not to forty people. But the truth is, this is far from guessing. It is "knowing that you know that you know"!

At a church in Philadelphia I pointed out a person by saying, "That woman in a red blouse who is fifty-nine years old back there." There were a thousand people present, so it was not easy to see the woman, but there she was. I said, "You have stage four cancer and the doctors expect you to die, but you want to live. God is healing you now." With that said, she trembled and cried with her hands to her face. She shook, then with the power of the Holy Spirit, God healed her and no one but Him laid a hand on her body to free her from the cancer. There are dozens of more examples. The point is with every word of knowledge, our God knows us. He knows every hair on our head. He knows everything about us.

In 1997 while I was ministering in a country church in Indiana, God would surprise us all again. During the service, I pointed out for healing a large man on crutches who was standing in the back of the church. The man's leg was injured in a motorcycle accident. I walked back to him and told him God was more interested in the state of his soul than He was in healing his leg. I told him he needed to get his life right with God. The big man looked sheepish at this point with his eyes downcast.

I told him that God could forgive his many sins. That he might know that God had the power to forgive his sins, I said to him, "God is going to heal your leg." I told him to drop his crutches and in the name of Jesus to walk. To everyone's amazement, the man walked pain free and healed by the power of God. I brought him to the front of the church for salvation. I asked the pastor to lead him in a prayer of forgiveness. Then he prayed for the man to be born again. When the prayer was finished, I spoke over the two men that this example of forgiveness of sin and physical healing would become a paradigm for the revival that was falling on this church in Indiana.

Many people would be coming here for God to change their former lives into something beautiful. I stretched out my hand over the two men and both of them were picked up off the floor by the power of God and flew back in the opposite direction until they fell on the carpet. The pastor was slain in the Spirit for over two hours. During that time, the glory of God filled the church. Little children, teenagers, mothers, and fathers wept and repented in the presence of God.

For months after, people were led by God to drive off the interstate between Indianapolis and Cincinnati, pull up to this church, which was kept unlocked during the day, and find the presence of the living God inside.

One example of restoration was the story of a mother and her daughter who came to the sanctuary. When they both stepped into the church, they grew uncomfortable and tried to leave for fear. As they reached the back door of the church, they could not get the doors open. Both were slain in the Spirit without any human being present. The girl was delivered from drug addiction, and the mother came under conviction for her many sins of not being there for her daughter and was forgiven.

MARINATING IN HIS PRESENCE

When I was a boy growing up, I'd spend time with my wonderful mother in the kitchen. I'd sit at the counter and we'd talk while she usually cooked or baked to feed nine hungry stomachs. One of my favorite dinners she prepared was London Broil, which we had on special occasions. I'd carefully watch mother as she scored the meat on both sides with a sharp knife leaving behind shallow cuts across the beef.

She would then place the meat in a container of marinade, which she made with extra virgin olive oil and sweet-smelling seasonings. The meat would sit in the marinade for several hours before it was broiled. Curious about the process, I questioned Mom about why the meat had to marinate for so long. She told me that this was the secret to a tasty, delicious London Broil. She explained that as the meat sat in the container of marinade, it took on the properties of the marinade. The marinade made the meat tender, juicy, and flavorful.

As we "marinate" in prayer in the presence of God, we take on the properties of God. His holiness and presence rubs off on us. We do not become holy and like God by trying harder to be like Him. This would be a work of the flesh. It must come with spending time with Him. I can thank God for some of my time in the seminary. It virtually was a monastery at the time; a place to carve out a deep well of prayer life before His presence and in His presence. It taught me one thing—to be comfortable in silence so I could learn to hear His voice.

John chapter ten says Jesus is the Good Shepherd. His sheep hear His voice; and the voice of another stranger His sheep will not follow. It is the voice of a loving Shepherd who lays down His life for His sheep. As you grow in relationship with God within, you will cultivate a place for hearing God. When you are baptized in the Holy Spirit, you will feel the well springing up in your belly, flowing with living waters. You, like me, will learn how to discern the voice of the Good Shepherd from the voice of the wolf leading you astray.

Moses went up the mountain to pray for forty days to be with God. As Moses marinated in the presence of His holiness, he became holy. When Moses came down from Sinai, his face glowed with a radiance of the presence of God. The radiance on his face frightened the people. To choose the holiness of God means to separate from the world. A clear division must occur between the secular and the holy. We are not different because of what we wear extrinsically as some religious sects. But we are different because of what we cling to intrinsically in Christ, putting on the new self. We become set apart by God and for God, though we are in the world but not of it. Paul puts it best when he states that we are consecrated to be *"a chosen people, a royal priesthood, a holy nation, God's special possession..."* (1 Pet. 2:9).

THE FIRST HEALING

I was in my eighth year of seminary when my little sister took ill after swimming in a pool. Suzie contracted meningitis and encephalitis, likely from a mosquito bite. It was at a time when she lay delirious in the hospital with her brain burning up at 106 degrees when neurologists saw no results from multiple antibiotics already used on the little eight-year-old girl.

At that time, I was about to be ordained and commissioned to begin ministering. I longed for God to heal my sister. He spoke to me that He would. I asked Him one thing—that I could be there at the hospital when Suzie's fever broke. She was restrained in the bed, her hands and her feet tied lest she hurt herself in a state of delirium. The doctors prepared my parents for the worst—death, blindness, or mental retardation.

I told my parents that God told me she would be healed on Monday morning and that I would be there to see the miracle. I asked them to come. Early Monday morning with a beautiful late summer sunshine filling the room, Suzie sat up in bed and said, "Hi Mommy, Hi Daddy, Hi Frank. Where am I?" Praise our God, she was perfectly normal again!

This first healing in my life took place because of faith in God; and faith in His promises that are always "Yes and Amen." No hands were laid on Suzie; no anointing was felt. Simply the prayer of a heartfelt seminarian who loved his sister, and who dared to believe in God more than to believe in a negative, yet realistic, medical report.

Preaching Worldwide

From 1994 on, I traveled around the United States preaching the good news and healing the sick in Jesus' name in many different churches. I also had many opportunities to preach in other nations around the world. One experience that I would like to share with you occurred in 2005 in the nation of South Korea.

I had gone to South Korea several times in the past. News of the anointing and impartation of the Holy Spirit was spreading throughout the country in Christian circles. So, the leadership there invited me to visit for about a month to preach in several of the larger churches throughout the land as well as in Seoul, the capital city. They also decided to invite 250 of the leading pastors in South Korea to come for a week-long seminar on healing and its place in revival. The last time South Korea had a revival was in the 1970s. This was over thirty years prior and things had died out. Church practices were back to business as usual and the excitement of the works of the Holy Spirit were not to be found anymore.

I realized that such an assignment would be a grueling task. If the Holy Spirit wanted me to spread revival throughout an entire nation and use me to do it, then I was going to be obedient.

I talked with the pastors of large church groups. Most were very open to the message of miracles; some didn't want change. But I always found the masses open to miracles and the power of God. When I prayed with an open pastor, the people were transformed before my eyes. It was also interesting to watch a dead church rise from its grave and be resurrected in three days by the Holy Spirit. This was all accomplished as I moved through the crowds laying hands and breathing the impartation upon anyone who was near. People fell down under the weight of the anointing, dozens at a time.

With many of the churches having well over 5,000 people in attendance, you may wonder, *How did he pray with so many people?* I really don't know other than the Holy Spirit imparted the anointing on me to give to tens of thousands of people. It was miraculous to behold.

There was one service in particular. I had just finished preaching and then praying with people for a good hour or two. I was drained. I thought I had nothing left to give. But the Holy Spirit was not finished yet. He told me there was one more, and that this one more was an exorcism.

He told me that there was a young woman present among the vast audience who had three problems. I told the people what the three problems were: she was into the occult as a witch of satan, she was drug-addicted, and she was a street prostitute.

Things got very awkward as time passed and no one came forward. Finally, the ushers got nervous and started to bring a few individuals to the front. I guess they didn't want the minister to look bad. But when a pastor calls out specific issues like I did, I knew God had someone in mind. I sent the ushers with their charges back to their seats.

I asked God where she was. He led me right to her on the right side of the vast auditorium. She was hiding on the floor away from view. The ushers finally saw her and picked her up and carried her forward. She arrived at the front and immediately slithered onto the floor and moved about like a snake. Her tongue was protruding out of her mouth and she hissed like a serpent right at me.

Everyone looked scared and no one approached her except me. I took authority in Jesus' name over the demonic powers. I bound them up and cast them out of her.

She wretched and vomited, then she cried like a baby. I spoke words of love and we sang a Korean song of love over her. She accepted forgiveness and allowed Jesus to send His Spirit into her. Her demonic tongue changed right away to a beautiful prayer language. I embraced her with a holy hug. The young woman was twenty-two years of age, but had looked to be closer to fifty. I had a prayer group of single women promise to take her into their group. I then told them to give her a Bible and to make sure she took Holy Communion to strengthen her frail body and soul. What struck me was that in spite of all the demons binding her life, there was still something inside that wanted God in the worst way. It was an amazing night in Seoul, South Korea.

Chapter 9

A PRIEST FOREVER

According to the Book of Hebrews, Jesus is not a descendent from the Levitical priesthood, like was John the Baptist, his cousin. So Jesus did not qualify for the role of cultic priest since He did not have a direct lineage to Aaron, the high priest. The law of Moses strictly rules that only male descendants of Aaron be commissioned to be priests in the Temple. Because John's father, Zechariah, was a priest in the line of Aaron, and Elizabeth, his mother, was likewise a descendent of Aaron, John the Baptist was actually the rightful choice as the Old Testament high priest at the time of Jesus. This duty was historically fulfilled by Caiaphas. He was appointed by the Roman government, with his only claim being the son-in-law of Ananias, the former Jewish high priest.

So what does this say of Caiaphas and John? It says Caiaphas had the political title but lacked the spiritual power from God; while John lacked the political title, but had the spiritual power from God. Be wary of those with title but lack the privilege. What is temporal and evident is not always true, spiritual authority. It is the function of the high priest to choose the lamb for sacrifice on the Day of Passover. This is why in the Gospel of Saint John, John the Baptist points out and chooses the Lamb of God as the sacrifice for Passover:

> *"The next day John saw Jesus coming toward him and said, 'Look, the Lamb of God, who takes away the sin of the world!"* (John 1:29).

Jesus descended through Mary from the line of David, the king of Israel and from the tribe of Judah. We know this because Mary, His birth mother, was from the genealogy related to David. We also know that Jesus was conceived through the power of the Holy Spirit, so Jesus is God, with God as His Father. This is the mystery of the Trinity. Jesus was a priest according to the order of Melchizedek.

The Book of Genesis states,

*"Then Melchizedek king of Salem brought
out bread and wine. He was priest of
God Most High, and he blessed Abram..."*
(Genesis 14:18-19).

Melchizedek means "King of righteousness" combining both the role of king and priest into one.

Psalm 110:4 mentions him again:

*"The Lord has sworn and will not change
his mind: 'You are a priest forever, in the
order of Melchizedek.'"*

This significance is that the Aaronic priesthood is destined to be set aside, while the order of Melchizedek's priesthood is to replace it for all eternity. When Jesus became our Lamb of sacrifice on the altar of Calvary, Jesus ended the need of a Jewish priesthood of Aaron or any other sacrificial priesthood as in the Roman Catholic church. This cultic need ceased with the death of Jesus as the Book of Hebrews states, *"Christ was sacrificed once to take away the sins of many"* (Heb. 9:28).

The priesthood according to the order of Melchizedek is superior to the Old Testament priesthood of Aaron and the tribe of Levi because of Jesus. The Book of Hebrews teaches us that Jesus was a priest according to the order of Melchizedek. By His perfect sacrifice offered, whoever accepts His gift of forgiveness also becomes a priest according to the order of Melchizedek.

So with this truth in mind, all of us who accept the gift of Christ's forgiveness now enjoy the positional role of members of a holy priesthood, a people set apart as Saint Paul teaches in the New Testament.

My personal identity changed from cultic priest as a Roman Catholic priest to blessed priest much like anyone accepting the gift of Jesus Christ. Leaving the cultic priesthood of the Roman Catholic church opened for me a new and better way through our only true High Priest, Jesus Christ. Along with this fundamental identity as "priest according to the order of Melchizedek," God gives us particular gifts, outlined in the Bible, to equip us in our particular role for Him.

PARTICULAR GIFTS

These gifts are different from talents that He also gives us. Talents are innate abilities like music, sports, or proficiency in a particular subject area like math or languages. The gifts are mentioned in Romans 12:6-8, which I call gifts from the Father; Ephesians 4:11-13, which I call gifts from the Son; and First Corinthians 12:4-11, which I call the gifts of the Holy Spirit. The natural gifts come at birth and include prophecy (speaking the truth), service, teaching, encouraging, giving, leadership, and mercy.

The five-fold anointing gifts are given to the church. These include apostles, prophets, evangelists, pastors, and teachers.

For our purposes, we will examine the third grouping or the gifts from the Holy Spirit. To make these nine gifts more understandable, I group them as:

Wisdom gifts

- Wisdom

- Word of knowledge

- Discernment of spirits

Power gifts

- Faith

- Healing

- Miracles

Word gifts

- Tongues

- The interpretation of tongues

- Prophecy

These gifts are given at the Baptism of the Holy Spirit, which is first evidenced by the gift of tongues. These are supernatural gifts. They are given by the Holy Spirit for supernatural works.

I encourage you to discover the gifts God has given to you. Know your gifts, because in knowing your gifts you will see much clearer your place in the world and in the church. You will know more clearly yourself and your personality. It is important to know both your strengths as well as your weaknesses: what gifts make you capable and qualified and what gifts do you need to depend on from someone in the Body of Christ?

This book has included an expose on my life in the ministry with an emphasis on the apostolic gift of healing and miracles. I realize that we are all unique, yet special in our own right unto God. One of my birth sisters is known by some as the "Mother Theresa of Philadelphia." She has worked tirelessly with other good, religious nuns as a Sister of Mercy on the streets of downtown Philadelphia with so-called "bag ladies." Her gift is clearly one of mercy and generosity. I marvel at what she has accomplished in people's lives.

I realize that I do not have these gifts that my sister has. I also realize we are both members of the Body of Christ. So, I can support her and encourage her and her ministry. She, on the other hand, does not have my gift of faith and miracles. She is not called as an apostle.

We have different gifts, yet we belong to one and the same Body in Christ. We have a different calling, yet one and the same Lord. We use our gifts for the good of the community at large. This is a beautiful aspect of the Body of Christ outlined by Saint Paul in the New Testament.

YOUR PARTICULAR GIFTS

I would like you to examine yourself. Ask God about your gifts. In particular, ask Him about your supernatural gifts. I find most charismatic individuals may see a strength in one or two supernatural charisms. What they don't realize is that the other supernatural gifts can come and be made manifest by stepping out and allowing the Holy Spirit to demonstrate the other gifts in them. It does take courage and it does take boldness. It may not be without its fears. Yet if you don't yield, they will not come. I encourage you to grow in the supernatural way of life. It is exciting.

After reading my words and stories in the Chapters of this book, some may say to themselves, "Dr. Sizer must be so special to be able to have so many experiences in the supernatural." It is true I do feel special, but I feel special because of the Spirit of Jesus living within me. To move in the life of the Holy Spirit is unique, special, and supernatural. To be able to hear God, and His will is unique, special, and supernatural.

I want this book to help you develop you on your own special journey with the Holy Spirit. I want you to be able to tell your own story of the Holy Spirit doing miraculous signs and wonders in your life. My purpose is to inspire you to see signs following them who believe.

Until recently we have only experienced brief flashes of God's brilliant power in the earth. We labor as it were to give birth to the wind (see Isa. 26:18). Yet, I do believe we are on the verge of seeing the greatest outpouring of the Spirit of God that the world will ever witness. We are living in a day when darkness is covering the earth, but the glory of God will make a blinding light.

The Book of Acts chapter 29 will be written by you and by me. God's power will be released in an apostolic way upon many. The apostolic age will require a new vision. The Holy Spirit will be poured out upon all flesh. Joel the prophet says that in those days:

> *Your sons and daughters will prophesy, your old men will dream dreams, your young men will see visions. Even on my servants, both men and women, I will pour out my Spirit in those days* (Joel 2:28-29).

Revival is coming. The real potential for changing a nation in a day will be possible. I saw a foretaste of what one man's faith can do while I was in South Korea, a few years ago. It will be accomplished by ordinary people like you and me joining our spirits with the power of the Holy Spirit. He will present us with new strategies and plans. He will open doors that the devil can't close, and He will close doors the devil can't open in those days. Millions upon millions will be saved. Atheists and agnostics will cry out, "Jesus is Lord!" Satanists will bow down before Jesus as Master Savior. Sin will give way to the Spirit; and His saving blood will set captives free. Muslims will witness the power of miracles and come to Jesus in scores and scores. Jews will call on the name of Yeshua.

EXTREME FAITH AND CONFIDENCE

You will become a burning stick snatched from the fire (see Zech. 3:2). You will have a strong sense of the headship of Jesus over your life. You will resist the approval of people, and claim no honors for yourself. You will recognize it is better to obey God than people, although there will exist in you no rebellion. You will simply be given over to the absolute Word and will of God. You will abandon everything in order to follow Him. You will be faithful in the smallest as well as the greatest tasks set before you by Him.

Such obedience is born out of extreme faith and confidence in the sovereign will of God. Your faith is in God alone regardless of the circumstances. Your confidence comes from the greater power of God at work in you. You will have more faith in the sanctifying work of the Holy Spirit than in the destructive work of the enemy. You live with no fear, save the fear of God Almighty.

You will not be religious. You will only be moved by relationship. You will be nonmaterialistic. For circumstances have caused you to be content whether you have or have not. You believe God provides. You think in terms of spirit, not in terms of flesh. You have become more eternal and less temporal. You will come to realize that all the supernatural gifts you are given are only a means for attaining the higher goal of Christ Jesus, your Lord.

Your concept of church will change because you will think no longer as a church having membership with walls; now you will be willing to go outside the camp with Christ, bearing reproach in order to find the lost. At times some of our churches have become like walled cities keeping out others unlike them. Your concept of churches will be safe havens of diversity, not social country clubs of superficial friendships.

The only wall you will be interested in is the wall of fire in Zechariah 2:5: *"And I myself will be a wall of fire around it,' declares the Lord, 'and I will be its glory within.'"* You will take on no honors for yourself, no longer will the church at large be filled with individuals with phony degrees and paper mill doctorates that the academic world laughs at. No longer will you need to feel like you need to be somebody you are not. These hypocritical people will be wiped aside. You will be authentic and honest with yourself. You will be nameless and faceless except in the name of Jesus.

No Other Name

You will gather in no other name but His. You will follow no other name but His. You will follow no other name but that of the Good Shepherd. You will agree to die to a personal agenda to follow Him. You will not allow yourself to be bought out by money, prestige, fame, or privilege. You are sold out to Christ alone. You will say what God says; and you will do what God does.

The driving force behind you will be the Holy Spirit prompting you to step in the way, "This is the way; walk in it." Living waters will flow out of your belly. You will not need to be prompted to praise God or to fast and to pray, these will be automatic and second nature to you. You will hear His voice; not the voice of another. You will know the sting of persecution, but you will focus rather on the blessings of God following. You will know the trials of life; but in resisting the devil, he will flee you.

We notice the world persecutes at times those who are saved. It mocks the believer led by the Holy Spirit. But it will hate and crucify the passionate, sold-out believer I am taking about. Those who have a form of godliness lack the power within. They are no threat to the kingdom of darkness. Only the type of follower that I outline here in these pages represents is the one who will deny self, take up the cross, and follow Him. These will be the threat to the enemy.

YOU ARE A FORERUNNER

The devil trembles with fear as the Holy Spirit prepares and calls forth you, forged in the likeness of John the Baptist. You will be a forerunner of Christ's second coming. You will prepare the way for the Lord. He will return as the Lion of the tribe of Judah. And you will become a consuming fire for God's purposes.

If this description of the end-time believer resonates with you, then you may very well be one chosen like me for this task. I believe Jesus is waiting for the church to rise up like true sons and daughters of the Almighty God. We together will be clothed like Elijah and John in nothing but the sheer power of God. It is true that my life has already seen a great deal of supernatural moves of God. But I do believe it is a foretaste of things to come.

A description of a radical believer in Jesus is hallmarked by a passionate love and trust in God to do something good in every situation. This attitude and conviction comes out of a kind of faith I read in John's gospel.

> *I tell you the truth, anyone who has faith in Me will do what I have been doing. He will do even greater things these, because I am going to the Father* (John 14:12).

Ever since I was called by the Holy Spirit to hold a Healing Service in 1976 I always made a point of having testimonies shared as the Service began. The reason was to give glory to the Lord and to raise up the faith of the people. The very first Healing Service the woman healed from stage four cancer dying in the hospital gave testimony. God was pleased with the encore and people were excited that what He did for her, He might do for them. But much more happened here. An environment or culture, if you will, of healing formed before our very eyes which expected God to act in everyone's behalf. The faith of the Body of Christ provided what I call a solidarity of belief in Christ. There was no room for doubt and unbelief; no room for fear of hesitation. Now, only faith could act.

We shall cast out demons and call down fire from heaven. Signs, wonders, and miracles will follow us. We will be baptized in repentance and baptized in fire. All of this will be done to the glory of God.

Let me give you an example to clarify what I am trying to say. I was doing ministry in Cape May, New Jersey . The chapel was built there by the entrepreneur John Wanamaker in the late nineteenth century for spiritual Revival.

The Seagrove Conference has been held in the Chapel every summer since for over one hundred years. I have had the privilege of speaking and praying for the sick there for over forty years of the hundred plus years. It is a joy to be there in this environment. The culture of Healing is deeply rooted. The expectations of God's hand moving in one's behalf is evident. The people are ready for miracles. Testimonies of healing are regular occurrence.

About ten years ago while moving about in the church doing ministry a strong commotion happened on the other side of the church. I quickly moved there to see what was the matter. An elderly man by the name of Lou apparently was found to be dead! His beloved wife Myrna was sobbing and shrieking. The pastor had his cell phone out prepared to call 911. Lou had no pulse and no heart beat. He had turned ashen grey and was cold to the touch. There was no sign of life. We had no medical team available so we had no physician confirm medical death. However, Lou was dead.

Today I joke that my sermon put Lou in such a deep sleep that he went on to be with the Lord. I gathered the believers around Lou and told them to pray for him to come back to life. Even Myrna had faith then to believe. I led the ten people in prayer and believed for resurrection power. I was unable to put my hand on Lou directly, but a young man Dave next to Lou could. He had his hand over Lou's heart and felt an electrical surge come through his hand into the dead man's heart. Lou immediately began to breath again and his color returned to his body. His wife's tears turned to joy at what the Lord had done for her. The power of the Body of Christ had moved into action. With God all things are possible. And through the Body of Christ greater things shall we do! Lou lived another ten years to be just shy of ninety years old this past year without any heath issues. He died in his sleep peacefully. We could have had the EMS come and take the dead body away after church. Instead we had coffee with Lou afterward knowing that Jesus is the Resurrection and the Life. Whoever believe in Him will live.

Great Days are coming to a people of faith. We shall caste out demons, call down fire from heaven, and even raise the dead back to life. Supernatural signs, wonders and miracles will follow us. We will be baptized unto repentance and baptized in the fire of the Holy Spirit. All of this will be done to the Glory of our God.

Chapter 10

FINAL WORD

The greatest take away from this book is my desire for you to see things differently. It involves seeing things from God's point of view; not from our point of view. This concept touches on the idea of living in the kingdom of God, which Jesus taught constantly. I mean, there is a natural and a supernatural way to live life. Even many believers in Christ live natural lives with a coating of religiosity thrown into the mix. They are led to believe they are living a supernatural life because they believe in a supernatural God. This is only partly the truth. We must not only *believe* in a supernatural God, but *enter into* the supernatural life! It is possible to do this through the Holy Spirit's power. To effectively live in the supernatural, we must be immersed by the fire of the Holy Spirit. This takes a power-encounter with God Himself.

I have lived on both sides of the equation. I know what it is like to be religious, having a form of godliness but lacking the power therein. This way of living is pious but in effect an ordinary life devoid of faith in supernatural expectations. Consequently, expectations when problems, difficulties, and infirmity come along are not much different from those in the world without Christ. These people seem to have hope at times, but not real faith in their prayers affecting a different, positive, supernatural outcome.

I know what it means to live supernaturally following a baptism of fire in the Holy Spirit. For me, this is the real deal and the only way to live. I wouldn't trade it to go back to the ordinary religious walk. It does come with a price because few chose to go after and pursue it. It can be lonely. It can bring persecution and ridicule. It does make you misunderstood. And it does cause you to be looked upon as out of the ordinary in a way that feels uncomfortable. But it is exciting because it means living, breathing God every day.

PERSONAL REVELATION

John is referred to as "the Revelator," since he wrote the Book of Revelation. The word "revelator" is telling. It is derived from the Greek words *apo,* which means "un" and *kaluptein,* which means "to cover. So apocalypse means to "uncover" or pull something back from someone. In this case, Jesus pulls back our shame and sin that covers every one of us born into this world. All the way back to Genesis 3:6 we see Adam and Eve covering themselves in their shameful sin and disobedience. For they sewed fig leaves as their eyes were opened to their sin and they covered themselves in shame.

Jesus came to restore our innocence by uncovering Himself as Love in the Bible and restoring us to innocence through Him. In the Book of Revelation he lays out a picture of Jesus. He unveils the divine nature of the person of Jesus. Though he walked with Jesus as a man and ate with Him and spoke to Him and saw that Jesus was fully human in every way, John "saw" with different eyes the divinity through the humanity. He grew to believe in the Word become flesh as he heard the words of God flow out of the person of Jesus Christ. John believed as he saw the miracles performed by the hands of Jesus. John believed as the words of Jesus were backed up by His behavior and acts.

It is revelation that enabled John to make this leap of faith about Jesus. Revelation 1:2 clearly lays out that an angel made known this revelation to John about Jesus. John simply testifies and bears witness to everything he saw. Romans 1:18 states that the truth about God is suppressed by the ungodly. It says that which is plainly seen from the beginning is imprinted upon humanity's consciences. But sin has blinded humankind to the self-evident fact that God is clearly discernable in all things in creation.

This same spiritual blindness that hinders people from seeing God in the universe, is the same spiritual blindness that hinders people from seeing God in Jesus Christ. It is the blindness of the Pharisee; the blindness of the know-it-all. Ironically, the imprint to see God is within everyone. But the light of faith must first remove the sin through humbling ourselves, seeking forgiveness for our pride, and throwing ourselves at the feet of the cross. It is only then that the light can help us to see.

In the story of healing the man born blind in John's Gospel, it is not the physical sight given to the blind man that is the greater miracle. It is not until Jesus confronts the man with the question, *"Do you believe in the Son of Man?"* He answers, *"Who is he, sir? Tell me so that I may believe in him."* Then the newly sighted man is given sight to really see. Jesus replies to him, *"You have now seen him; in fact, he is the one speaking with you"* (John 9:35-37). With this exchange, the natural gives way to the supernatural; the light overshadows the darkness. The revelation of the Word opens the spirit of the man to see.

Our journey in Jesus takes us on a path that will forever change our ability to see. Through following the truth of the Holy Spirit, we find greater challenges and eventually answers to these challenges. Being immersed in the Holy Spirit presents opportunities for greater encounters with God—and growth in His Holy Spirit. This is the place where this book was birthed—in the Holy Spirit. The release of the Holy Spirit in His magnificent awe and majesty with our spirit explodes like a nuclear bomb and touches not only our spirit but also our mind, our heart, and our body. Like the Big Bang, it flows ever outward in ripples of concentric circles and waves of liquid love. Whatever it touches and whomever it touches is dramatically changed by the supernatural realm of God. There is no other explanation.

This is what happened to me. This is what can happen to you.

I see the Lord preparing the Church to follow Him in a special way these days. He is presenting many, many opportunities to people to come and follow Him in a deeper way. He wants to equip the Church and to impart new realms and experiences with the Holy

Spirit. New dimensions never before witnessed by God's people lie before them. His call goes out to all desiring to be consecrated in holiness and what is right. This call is to be carried by believers to the ends of the earth. In this age, God's economy of things and His priorities must take precedence over all other things.

In 1983, while I was in a spirit of prayer, the Holy Spirit put the following words upon my heart:

> *Draw close to Me, and I will draw close to you. Renew the joy of your salvation daily.*
>
> *Seek to get My Word ever deeper into your heart. Empty yourself of the things of this world, and fill yourself with the things of God. I must come ahead of all others.*
>
> *Trust in Me must come ahead of all others. My truth must lead you. It must come ahead of all opinions. Do not justify things that God says are wrong.*
>
> *Do not call what God calls "good," not good. Do not call what God calls "not good," good.*
>
> *Take care not to allow yourself to be compromised. Beloved, I have called you into the Light and Truth. The blind cannot lead the blind. Follow what I tell you by My Holy Spirit.*

Pray without ceasing. Do not allow yourself
to be anxious for anything. Stay alert; for
the appointed time is at hand.

These words have greatly impacted me. I hope they have a similar effect on you as well. It seems as though God wants us all to use our time on earth to draw near to Him and to be used to draw others to Him. It is a mission in which nothing else really seems to matter to Him.

A FAITHFUL REMNANT

He wants to empty us of the things of this earth that are only temporal and passing. He wants to fill us with the things that are eternal. Many in the Church have been led astray by false prophets teaching a prosperity gospel that is questionable to the message of the cross. God is not interested in the kind of car we drive as long as it gets us there, supplying our needs.

In the past decade, many believers have been led astray by teachers of dominion theology in charismatic circles, which has dubious support in the Word of God about these days before Christ's return. The Bible is clear that God is not especially interested in taking over politics or the economy or Hollywood. Jesus refused to do it during His public ministry saying "His Kingdom was not of this world". As a matter of fact, Jesus resisted these things as some wanted to make Him King. What

God is really interested in is the salvation of people and living right before Him. Once people come to Jesus as Savior and Lord their life values will undoubtedly influence cultures. In the end times He tells us there will be only a remnant faithful to Him. Our role as His faithful followers is to spread and live the gospel before all peoples to the ends of the earth. Yes, I do believe a Great Revival is about to explode on the earth's stage. With it will come an outpouring of unbelievable mercy and grace. People from all over the world will be affected by the Great Revival. Then He shall return.

There is a sense of urgency in His words. It is as though the time is short before He returns. Like the hound of heaven, He pursues us to come and follow Him. God seems that He is not satisfied with us simply being born again. He wants all of us, every part of us.

I am reasonable enough to recognize that there are different degrees of calling and different degrees of mission for every one of Christ's followers. Each one of us must be honest and open with Him to discern how we are to serve and follow the Lord. What is important here is that we be in the will of God and not step outside of what He calls us to do. For example, not everyone is called to sell everything they possess to follow Christ. Material things were the impediment for the young, rich man and Jesus knew this (see Matt. 19:23). Not all of us are called to be full-time ministers traveling as evangelists. To each is given a specific call and purpose. To each is given specific gifts and talents. It is for us to discover our call, our gifts, and our talents to be used properly in our lives.

But to those of us who have the fire of God burning in their bellies, I say, "Follow Him." For to pursue the Lord God alone, to set Him above all other priorities in life, is more rewarding than any other life there can be found. Just as Jesus acknowledged Mary and her prayer life above her sister Martha and her good housekeeping, God sees the ultimate purpose for us to be in relationship with Him. Being God's portion and inheritance is more rewarding than any other lifestyle.

The Book of Joshua records that the Israelites receive their inheritance in the land of Canaan. God had given Moses instructions as to how to divide the land among the twelve tribes. Joshua assigned the allotments from the directives of Moses. Every tribe received a portion of the land, that is, except the tribe of Levites. This is significant. The Levites were the priestly tribe that pressed into the Holy of Holies within the Tabernacle. They, above all other tribes, had a reverence and understanding for the holy vessels of God. So God deliberately doesn't give them a portion of the land but allows them to live wherever in the Promised Land. He tells them that *"the priestly service of the Lord is their inheritance"* (Josh. 18:7). God then says something to them that is even more stunning. He says, *"I am your share and your inheritance"* (Num. 18:20).

By living in deep, intimate relationship with God, the Levites led the peoples of the other tribes in a supernatural walk before God. They were, in effect, richer and more blessed in life than all other people. They were never found in a state of lack or need. They lived in abundance through the generosity of the tithes and offerings of the other tribes. For whenever we make God our treasure, we possesses all there is to possess.

Jesus did many other signs in the presence of many believers at healing services, in hospitals, in private residences, in public places, and in prayer meetings. These are not recorded in this book, *Power Encounters*. But the ones recorded in this book are written that you may believe that Jesus is the Christ, the Son of God, and that by believing you may have life in His Name. If you are among those readers who have never seen a miracle, fear not. The Lord has beautiful sentiments toward you. For He says, *"Blessed are those who have not seen and yet have believed"* (John 20:29). But if you are among those who have witnessed miraculous, **Power Encounters** at work in your life, count yourself privileged. For you, like me and like John the beloved apostle, have seen the Risen Lord and the supernatural work of the Holy Spirit.

ABOUT THE AUTHOR

Dr. Francis J. Sizer was ordained as a Roman Catholic Priest following eight years of study. He served in the Archdiocese of Philadelphia for over eight years. He then broadened his ministry to all denominations as a Healing Evangelist. He holds three accredited Masters degrees and a Doctoral degree from the University of Maryland. He is a licensed Clinical Psychologist and is Board Certified in the states of Ohio and Pennsylvania. He ministers in healing—physical, emotional, and spiritual.